Foreword

Five years ago, environmental building design was a freakish business, carried out by a handful of dedicated designers with little or no information to help in their work. Five years on, much has changed. Environmental issues are often the norm – for example about a third of all UK office designs are assessed using the BREEAM environmental assessment method. To the familiar litany of 'what material? what cost? what reliability?' the designer is now adding 'what environmental consequence?'.

Up to now, the designer has had little help in making an environmental choice. Environmental effects are complex and difficult to compare, and many of the consequences are still being debated. Faced with these problems, even the most dedicated designer has problems of selecting the most appropriate components and materials.

This book is therefore greatly welcomed, because it is the first really practical handbook for designers to make environmental preferences. Clearly, page by page, for each building component, it spells out the choices facing the designer and helps them in making the best environmental choices while avoiding the worst options.

Unsurprisingly, the concept originated in the Netherlands, where the population is faced daily with environmental disaster if they fail adequately to understand and respect the world about them. Consequently, the Dutch have led many of the environmental initiatives in Europe, and this handbook is one of them. Dutch realism and pragmatism are reflected in the easy way of using the handbook. Preferences are laid out very clearly; the environmentally most preferable choice is on the left-hand side of the page, When in doubt, it's easy to make the best environmental choice, simply by selecting the preference nearest to the left-hand margin. Drive on the left – it's that simple.

In travelling round the world, I am struck by the sameness of building processes and components. Everywhere a tap is a tap, a spade a spade. So although many specifics in this handbook apply to northern Europe, much of its content is applicable in all countries and in all continents.

The Environmental Preference Method concentrates on the consequences of selecting building materials and components. It therefore complements other environmental schemes such as BREEAM, which focus more on the effects arising during the building's use.

Altogether, this is an excellent handbook, and I thoroughly recommend its use.

JOHN DOGGART
ECD Energy & Environment Limited

5

Part I

Background to sustainable building in practice

1. Introduction

Why sustainable building?
Sustainability is an issue of great importance for society, and for the building sector:
50% of material resources taken from nature are building-related.
Over 50% of national waste production comes from the building sector.
40% of the energy consumption in Europe is building-related.

Designers of buildings and their service systems play a key role within the building sector. Consciously or not, they regularly choose between alternatives with a greater, or lesser, environmental impact. For real, informed choices to be made, it is essential that these professionals have insight into the relative environmental impact of the options open to them.

Reliable details on the environmental effects of building materials and certain technical operations are not freely available. Up to now the environmental profiles of individual products and processes have mainly been identified by means of Life Cycle Analysis (LCA) studies, which map out the environmental effects of a particular material, from extraction through to production, use, demolition and recycling. However, there is already substantial agreement that LCA is not suitable for comparing choices in the design process of buildings, moreover, most building products have not yet been investigated in this way. Further, these studies do not tell us how to evaluate one kind of environmental impact against another – for instance, what is more important (in the long and short term), destruction of tropical rain forests or destruction of the ozone layer?

Definite answers to such questions are not likely to be available in the short term. The experiments on which this handbook is based are, however, characterised by a pragmatic approach, based on such information as is available. The Environmental Preference Method (EPM), is a successful, practical tool for comparative assessment of environmental impact in the design process, and for making informed choice.
The Environmental Preference Method was developed in1991 by Woon/Energie (now W/E) within the framework of SEV's programme on sustainable living. SEV is the Dutch 'Steering Committee on Experiments in Housing'. While acting as consultants on several sustainable building projects the company learned there was a great demand for easily accessible and up-to-date information on the environmental impact of building components and materials.

The Environmental Preference Method – in brief
The Environmental Preference Method compares materials and products currently on the market and ranks them according to their environmental impact. A preference ranking has been developed for each of the construction elements in a building, ranging from wall construction through to waterproof membranes used in a roof, through to kitchen units. (Rankings have been applied to both new construction and refurbishment work.) Considerations such as cost or aesthetics are not involved in this assessment. The result is not an absolute assessment but a relative ranking based on environmental impact: an environmental preference.
However, recognising that the ideals of the environmental preference are not always attainable, the method also provides what could be termed a 'best practical solution' (the *basic selection*). When preparing a specification, the architect, engineer or contractor can quickly refer to this manual for the preferred environmental solution.

In brief, the Environmental Preference Method considers environmental impact throughout the whole life cycle of a material or product, during the extraction phase (raw material), production phase, building phase, occupational phase, and decomposition phase (see p.12). The main issues considered in the assessment are:
– shortage of raw materials
– ecological damage caused by extraction of raw materials
– energy consumption at all stages (including transport)
– water consumption

- noise and odour pollution
- harmful emissions, such as those leading to ozone depletion
- global warming and acid rain
- health aspects
- risk of disasters
- repairability
- reusability
- waste

So far, the Environmental Preference Method has proved to be a very successful tool. Over 50% of the local authorities in the Netherlands use the original Dutch version of this handbook to draw up building guidelines. EPM is also being used as an evaluation tool in seven EU Member states, for example in Thermie Building targeted projects, such as Energy Comfort 2000 projects. In the Netherlands, a large building products retailer has its line of products screened yearly using this method. In Poland an adaptation to the Polish construction market has been developed.

Environmental Preference Method and the future

The Environmental Preference Method is not static. Our considerations are based on information available at the time of writing, so subsequent research data may affect environmental preferences and therefore also this handbook. There is another way in which this handbook may be affected: the development of new products and markets is being stimulated by the fact that many project managers are already taking environmental preference into account in their choice of materials. Manufacturers will continue to bring new, cheaper or less environmentally damaging alternatives onto the market. Any handbook such as this, therefore, can only reflect the current situation.

The basic selection is also liable to change for the same reasons. Rising demand may lead to a fall in the price of some currently expensive alternatives (this has been the case for many less environmentally damaging building materials during recent years). The quality of some products is also likely to improve with increasing practical experience.

This handbook is a working resource for today, but work is already in hand to expand and refine the information it contains, for the future, and to cover commercial and public building. W/E are carrying out new projects to elaborate further the application of design tools for buildings. In the future the environmental preferences will be tested by sensitivity analysis. Ongoing projects are the EU project REGENER under the APAS programme, the method ECO QUANTUM in the Netherlands and BE^{2}AM under the Thermie B-programme. Major work has to be done, so that reliable European databases of industrial production processes can be developed as a basis for full integration of environmentally conscious design in the building process.

Structure of the handbook

In the first section of this handbook we touch on sustainable building in practice. The policies adopted and the Environmental Preference Method are fully explained. Parts 2 and 3 map out the environmental selection of materials for use in construction and refurbishment. The fourth and last part of the handbook provides environmental information about a large number of materials used in the building industry.

Responsibility for choice

It is down to those who commission buildings, to developers, councils, housing associations and the building sector itself to put in place sound environmental policies at a local level. In some countries policy instruments such as regulations and subsidies are absent, and it may not yet be possible to lay down statutory conditions for sustainable building. Yet this does not reduce the responsibility carried by all parties involved in new-build and refurbishment to reduce the risks their choices impose on human beings and the environment.

2. Sustainable building in practice

The main 'flows' through a building are of energy, water and materials. This handbook focuses mainly on the material strategy, though energy and water 'flows' are taken into account, where applicable.

Integrated life cycle management and sustainable building
Integrated life cycle management means striving to keep raw materials within a single cycle as much as possible. This means a minimum of waste, lengthening the life span of building components, increasing the flexible use of dwellings, and promoting the recycling of materials and products after the demolition of the building. This prevents the depletion of raw materials, which are becoming scarce in the long-run, and it limits the negative environmental impact which can appear over the whole life cycle of any material.
All raw materials used in construction are released again in one form or another at the time of demolition. We must strive for a high-grade reuse of these waste materials. For instance, concrete rubble from demolition waste is regarded as the preferred product for manufacture of new concrete, and the reuse of an aluminium window frame is preferable to smelting the frame down and processing it into a new product.

The ultimate aim is to integrate the life cycle as much as possible. The basic strategy for choice of sustainable building materials consists of the following steps:
– prevention of unnecessary use and efficient use of materials
– use of renewable and recycled sources
– selection of materials with the least environmental impact.

Step 1 Prevention of unnecessary use and efficient use of materials
While in some industries, such as the packaging industry, the quantity of material used is an economic, political and environmental issue, in the building sector such material efficiency is not get an integral part of discussions on the environmental impact of buildings.
Yet any client, investor or governmental body could thoroughly evaluate the need for new construction activity. It is at the early design phase, especially, that significant improvements can be achieved, for instance, by investigating the possibilities for renovation and reuse of existing buildings. Secondly, designers can design a building to be as efficient as possible, by minimising the resources needed (this can be done by optimising the floor plan and construction). In the final design and specification phase an optimisation of the sizes of components may be helpful to avoid demolition waste during construction. Last, the expected lifetime of a component should be adjusted to its technical lifetime.

Step 2 Use of renewable and recycled sources
By making use of renewable and recycled sources the life cycle of building materials can be closed. Renewable sources will be reproduced by nature during the lifetime of the material. Recycled materials will enter a second life, without taking resources from nature.
Apart from application of renewable and recycled products, clients and designers can allow for future recycling by
– not using composite materials that cannot be separated at the end of the life cycle
– not glueing and sealing components together
– designing buildings for dismantling, not for demolition.
However, it is important to consider the sustainability of the renewable sources. For most types of European wood and agricultural products such as flax, there is no immediate concern. Most types of tropical wood, however, are not sustainably reproduced. When applying materials from renewable sources it is important to design in a way that harmful preservatives are avoided.
Recycled products are reproduced from existing building materials or from by-products of other industrial sectors. The best recycling is direct reuse of components or complete

buildings. When talking about recycled products one should consider the fact that the share of recycled material in new products may vary from very low percentages up to 100% recycled material.

A second consideration is the quality and use of the recycled product. The so-called down-cycling into low grade applications will not close the life cycle, but only expand lifetime.

One should take care with the application of other sectors' waste, because of eventual contamination of building products.

Step 3 Selection of materials with the least environmental impact
The environmental impact of materials is caused during the complete lifetime. Typical environmental issues are: raw materials, embodied energy, emissions, hindrance, waste, recycling, repair and lifetime. It is important to select those building products which have the lowest environmental impact.

More efficient use of energy
In promoting the efficient use of energy one is aiming for a reduction in the consumption of finite energy sources, such as coal, oil and natural gas. This breaks down into the need to undertake the following steps:

– reduce the demand for energy
– increase the use of renewable energy
– increase energy efficiency.

In formulating future savings targets for space heating, it is recommended that existing houses be completely or additionally insulated. Measures should also be taken with regard to heating systems, such as the replacement of existing boilers with condensing boilers and the use of heat recovery and solar heating systems. Part of the savings can come from combined heat and power, and district heating. Energy-saving measures can also be undertaken when necessary maintenance is carried out.

Promotion of quality
Life cycle control and a more efficient use of energy are both forms of quality promotion. The focus here is specifically on the indoor environment and the environmental value of the residential area. The subjects concerned are:
– the indoor environment (sound insulation, absence of radon, economic ventilation, combustion equipment, the exclusion of asbestos)
– raising the quality of the residential area
– raising the quality of building materials.

Sustainable new construction
The focus in sustainable building ranges from the environmentally sound integration of dwellings into the surrounding residential area to the drawing up of a specification in such a way that the future, high-grade reuse of building components is possible. The main thing is to keep both the short and long-term impact on the environment to a minimum.

Sustainable refurbishment
The prime motivation in sustainable refurbishment lies in the need to contain the negative environmental impact of refurbishing. The refurbishing process in particular offers an additional opportunity to combat existing environmental problems, usually with regard to the interior. These include:
– noise pollution caused by traffic and neighbours
– emissions of hazardous substances in the ground under suspended floors
– emissions of hazardous substances from existing construction materials the presence of asbestos
– high energy consumption for heating
– poor ventilation which impairs the quality of the indoor environment
– cold bridges in the construction, which lead to the formation of mould and damage to the building.

3. Environmental preference methodology

Goal and result

The Environmental Preference Method was developed by Woon/Energie (now W/E) in 1991. Experience as consultants on several sustainable building projects showed there was a great demand for accessible and up-to-date information on the environmental impact of building components and materials.

A ranking of building materials according to environmental preference, following the typical building patterns in the Netherlands, could meet this need. In order to establish this ranking a method was required that could transform a wide range of information into an easy, comprehensible assessment in a limited amount of time and allow for the assessment to be changed in the light of new information.

The method aims to compare available materials and products and rank them according to environmental preference. Other considerations such as cost or aesthetics are not involved in this assessment. The result is not an absolute assessment but a relative ranking based only on environmental impact: an environmental preference.

This chapter elaborates two major aspects of the Environmental Preference Method (EPM): the structure of the Environmental Preference Assessment and the application of the results.

Structure of the Environmental Preference Assessment

The EPM follows the same structure as a LCA (Life Cycle Assessment as formulated by CML Leiden, the Netherlands) but in a simplified way.

The entire life cycle is considered, i.e. from extraction of the raw material through to processing the waste material at the end of the component's life.

EPM can be considered as a combination of 'global analysis' and 'problem analysis'. That means that all relevant aspects are taken into consideration, but based on available information (not necessarily in quantitative data). Aspects which are expected to have an extremely large impact or a potential for improvement are more thoroughly investigated. In this way all relevant differences will quickly emerge.

Comparison per functional unit

Comparisons have been made by taking a building component with a certain lifetime as the functional unit, instead of a kilogram or cubic metre of a particular material. The damage caused to the environment by insulation material, for instance, is calculated using the amount of insulation material required to insulate $1m^2$ of floor surface area with a particular insulation value. In making such assessments, judgements have to be made concerning the relative importance of different issues.

Life cycle

Impact on the environment over the whole life cycle must come into a judgement of environmental preference. Listed below are several distinct phases and the most important environmental issues they raise:

1. Extraction phase

The stock of raw material which can be extracted is judged on technical, economic and environmental factors. Some materials will be depleted within the foreseeable future if the present scale of extraction continues. Zinc, lead and gravel, for instance, will be depleted within decades at the current rate of use. The extraction of raw materials often results in damage to nature (for instance when tropical hardwoods and bauxite are extracted), in the release of harmful emissions (from coal mining) or in the risk of an environmental disaster (the extraction and transportation of oil and chlorine).

2. Production phase

During this phase the raw materials are processed, resulting ultimately in a material or product. Problems during this phase include harmful emissions into soil, air and water, as well as the creation of waste, and energy consumption. In general, the more processing involved, the more the environment will be threatened.

3. Building phase

The most important environmental problems occurring during the building phase are the consumption of energy and the creation of waste and pollution (noise, vibration, dust). However, care taken during building influences the life span of the various building elements, as well as the life span of the overall structure.

4. Occupational phase

Environmental damage during this phase is determined to a large extent by choices made in earlier phases. Here we are concerned with the impact of these choices on the health of the occupants in the form of emissions of noxious substances from building materials (e.g. chipboard, phosphogypsum, paints and adhesives) and problems relating to the quality of the indoor environment (damp, draughts, noise pollution). On the other hand, pollution also results from the use of dwellings, such as water and energy consumption, decorating and the creation of household waste.

5. Decomposition phase

A large amount of rubble is created through demolition during the decomposition phase. Refurbishment or maintenance extends the life span of the dwelling, and waste is only created from a fraction of the building components and materials. The impact on the environment of demolition waste is great, however, taking the form of harmful emissions to the air (incineration), and water and soil (landfill). For recycling, it is important for the materials to be well separated and clean. Primary reuse – that is, instances where building components are used again in the same or in other houses, following minimal reprocessing if necessary – is preferable.

Assessment procedure

The procedure of Environmental Preference Assessment contains the same four steps as a LCA: goal definition, inventory, classification and evaluation.

Step 1 Goal definition

The first step is an inventory of the available alternatives in the choice of materials and defining the functional units and amount of material required for a particular application. For each building element a review has been undertaken to identify the various materials or products that would normally be used. For example, window frames might either be preservative-treated softwood, untreated softwood, temperate hardwood, tropical hardwood, aluminium or PVC.

Step 2 Inventory

The second step is an inventory of the environmental effects of each alternative based on available information. These effects can be described through quantitative or qualitative data and are, for example, the use of resources or energy, release of emissions and production of waste. Available information can consist of LCAs already carried out, data provided by manufacturers and other surveys.

Step 3 Classification

The effects are translated into assessments on the five main, relevant environmental aspects: resources, energy, emissions, damage and waste. (Emissions due to use of energy belong to the aspect 'energy'.) Three other features are also taken into consideration: re-usability, repairability and life span. The alternatives are compared by building a matrix on each aspect/feature by means of assigning plus-signs, zero or minus-signs and an x-sign if the effect is very harmful.

Step 4 Evaluation

This matrix is the basis for determining the environmental preference of the possible options. There is no fixed weighting of the scores for each aspect as their relevance is not the same for every application. For example: the use of resources will be more important when comparing alternatives for the main construction, while emissions will be more important when comparing alternatives for paintwork. Subjective decisions had to be made by those reviewing the data.

14

Applications of the results

The handbook gives a brief description of the environmental considerations that resulted in their ranking. This simple ranking of product types allows environmental concerns to play a role with other factors, such as price and durability, in the decision-making process. When preparing a specification, the architect, engineer or contractor can quickly refer to the manual for the preferred environmental solution.

A large retail company in building materials in the Netherlands has its line of products screened yearly by using this method. So far it has appeared to be a very successful tool. In Poland an adaptation to the Polish construction market has been developed. The Environmental Preference Method is also being used as an evaluation-tool in seven EU countries, e.g. in Thermie Building targeted projects, such as Energy Comfort 2000.

4.   Background to EPM in the Netherlands

In the Netherlands, the political background for this handbook was established by the 'National Environmental Plan' (NMP) and the explanatory note on 'Sustainable Building' published in the early 1990s. More recently agreement has been reached between government and the building industry on the main environmental issues, such as resources, energy (including related emissions), other release of emissions and production of waste.
Alternatives need to be sought when attempting to restrict the negative environmental aspects of construction and refurbishment.

Experimental projects and pilot studies relating to new-builds and the refurbishment of existing dwellings have been conducted in the Netherlands. They were aimed at applying the theory of sustainable building in practice. The handbook is based on the results of these projects. Both the original and this handbook are based on the evaluation of a large number of practical experiments and pilot projects supported by the Dutch organisation SEV (Steering Committee on Experiments in Housing) within the framework of the Schoner Wonen (sustainable living) experimental programme.

This Environmental Preference Method was first published in the Netherlands by SEV. In 1991 the rankings for the refurbishment of domestic dwellings were published, and in 1993 those for new construction and refurbishment. Over 50% of local authorities in the Netherlands have now used the handbook to draw up guidelines.

The *Construction* section is based on several trials, to name but a few: Bloemendaal (The Hague), Ecolonia (Alphen aan de Rijn), both in the Netherlands, and Schafbrühl (Tübingen) in Germany.

Most of the pilot studies are based on the requirement for sustainable building to be achieved within existing budgets and this has usually proved possible. However extra subsidies were available to cover the additional costs of specific provisions, such as solar heaters and equipment for the collection and use of rainwater, and proved to be a good incentive.

The SEV supported and evaluated refurbishment projects. Typical Dutch examples are: Jan Evertsenstraat (Amsterdam), De Straat (Spangen Rotterdam) and Landsherenkwartier (Deventer).
The results of these projects have been incorporated in the *Refurbishment* section. The environmental measures which were employed varied: some projects contained many radical measures which incurred hefty additional costs, while others were more modest. In general however a good overview of current opportunities for completing refurbishment in a sustainable fashion has been achieved. Refurbishment can in itself offer an opportunity to select a less environmentally-damaging variant.

In the Netherlands a method has been developed to check the calculated energy consumption of a dwelling against the maximum energy performance allowed for that dwelling. This method – called energy performance standardisation (EPN) – was introduced in 1995. New houses now have to meet an energy performance standard for space heating, domestic hot water, and supplementary energy for heating and ventilation. The standard is set by the Dutch Ministry of Housing, Physical Planning and the Environment. The duty to check that its standards are maintained is soon to fall into hands of the local authorities, which give planning permission. Such a system could also be created elsewhere.

A Europe-wide perspective

Though developed initially in the Netherlands, the Environmental Preference Method is now in use as an evaluation tool in seven EU countries, for example in Thermie Building targeted projects such as Energy Comfort 2000 and European Housing Ecology Network. Experience has demonstrated that substantial parts of the rankings are applicable throughout Europe.

We are aware, however, that there will be specific cases in which regional conditions or building practices will suggest an environmental preference or basic selection that varies from the one given. Similarly, users of this handbook outside Europe will be aware of environmental preferences in need of modification (sources of timber, to name one example).

An adaptation to the Polish market has already been produced. In time, we expect more such adaptations to be developed, using the Environmental Preference Method. These will allow for regional differences or regional variations in environmental data for building products.

5. Relevant environmental issues

This chapter elaborates on the various environmental issues involved in the comparison of building products to be found in Part 2 *Construction* and Part 3 *Refurbishment*. An important point to observe when comparing these issues is whether the damage to the environment can be repaired through human intervention and the time-scale that would be involved. Environmental, technical and political manageability are also important factors. In general, the extent of the problem becomes greater as its scale increases. The greenhouse effect and damage to the ozone layer can be seen as more important than localised soil pollution or noise nuisance.

Damage to ecosystems
An ecosystem is the symbiosis between living (plants and animals) and non-living entities (e.g. soil, climate) in a particular area. Harm can be done both to our ecosystem and landscapes. It may take from decades to centuries for the balance to be restored in an ecosystem which has been disrupted.

Scarcity of resources
By scarcity of resources we mean that the ratio of available stock to consumption is such that supply is threatened in the short term. The available supply may be much smaller than the true existing stock for environmental, economic or technical reasons.

The stock of many raw materials is finite. As replenishment of the stock is an extremely slow process (in some cases thousands of millions of years) the stock could become depleted. Renewable raw materials are regenerated much faster because the material is produced by living organisms. Oil, coal and gas are also formed by living organisms, but it takes millions of years before these organisms are converted to useful raw materials. We can only speak of a renewable raw material therefore when the rate at which the raw material increases (turnover rate) is of a comparable order to that of the rate of consumption. At the present high consumption of raw materials that means a turnover rate of 1–100 years.

Emissions
Noxious substances can be released during the whole course of a material's life. These include the emission of harmful solid, fluid or gaseous substances to soil, water or air. Examples are heavy metals from wood preservatives, zinc leachate from roof coverings and CFCs (which damage the ozone layer) from insulation materials.

Disasters can happen during the extraction, transport, storage, production and use of certain materials, Normally the risk of these occurring is very small, but should a disaster strike, the consequences for people and the environment would be colossal. This may be a reason for including even a small risk of disaster as an important environmental aspect to consider in choosing building materials.

Energy use
Energy use means not only energy consumed during production, but also during extraction and transport. Energy use in itself signifies the consumption of scarce raw materials on the one hand, and the emission of harmful substances which contribute to the greenhouse effect (CO_2), acid rain (NO_x and SO_2) and smog (NO_x and hydrocarbons) on the other.

Waste
When a product has fulfilled its function, the resulting waste may cause numerous problems, including difficult separation, poor degradability, airborne dust, occupation of space or leaching in landfill, as well as the release of noxious substances incineration. If waste enters the environment after the demolition of a building, either through landfill or in another way, then the environmental pollution created will depend on the particular combination of the material's ability to cause harm and its degradability. The waste could either take up space,

which is also negative, or have damaging effects over a shorter time period if it degrades well.

Reuse

Reuse can be promoted in two ways in sustainable building: in the first place, by selecting products which can be reused in a primary (unchanged) or secondary fashion (where the by-product is used as raw material for making building materials), and secondly by choosing products which can be used again after demolition.

Reuse results in less waste and a reduction of the consumption of raw materials, but the environment gains most from primary reuse, where the waste does not require reprocessing to create the new product.

Life span and repairability

Greater durability results in fewer repairs to a product and obliterates the need for replacement later on, so that the burden on the environment over a certain period is reduced. It is, though, important for the durability of individual building elements to match the life span of the whole building. This will often be a shorter period for refurbishment, than it would for a new-build. Good degradability of waste after demolition is important, unless the waste is suitable for primary or secondary reuse.

Environmental effects of commonly used building materials

The environmental impact of a number of commonly used building materials is detailed in Part 4, and it has been taken into account when determining the environmental preference in Parts 2 and 3. The building element data sheets focus on comparing the applications.

6. Using the handbook

Parts 2 and 3 of the handbook, *Construction* and *Refurbishment,* are designed as reference material, and form the core of the handbook. Alternative design solutions are indicated for different building elements, as well as the materials which can be used. We have ranked these alternative solutions according to environmental preference, with the least environmentally damaging alternative on the left and the most environmentally-damaging choice on the right (see example below). *least ← → most damaging*

Ground under suspended floors	preference 1 shells	preference 2 foamed concrete, sand	preference 3 expanded clay granules, PE membrane	not recommended PVC membrane

This gives a quick overview of the preferred choice of materials and makes the handbook an appropriate tool for members of a building team preparing plans for construction or refurbishment. Part 2 gives preferences for building elements used in new construction and Part 3 for those used in refurbishment.

Building element data sheets
The building elements have been divided into a number of separate components. For instance, the roof has been divided into sections on shape, construction, joints and insulation. For each component we give the main environmental preference, followed by a justification and comments, as well as an indication of cost.

An environmental preference consists of a range of appropriate product-alternatives for the building element concerned. The ranking is explained in pp. 12–14 of this manual, the *Environmental preference methodology*. Environmental issues *only* have been taken into account. Other issues, such as cost and appearance, have not been considered, unless they affect the environment such as the need for maintenance and durability. We have also noted alternatives which threaten the environment to such an extent that they are not recommended. Although we have made a purely objective judgement, the ranking in the *not recommended* category does depend on the existence of suitable alternatives. The adoption of a given material must meet the requirements of building regulations.

Relative evaluation
Various alternatives for each building component are compared.
We stress, however, that we are dealing with a relative assessment of the materials. Alternatives for each are listed, and then the environmental impact is considered.
That a material exerts a seriously harmful effect in just one environmental category may be decisive enough for that material not to be recommended for a particular application, especially where sufficient alternatives are available. (In the future we plan to test the environmental preferences with a sensitivity analysis.) We have used a considerable number of printed sources for the evaluation of environmental impact, and our bibliography is listed in the Dutch edition.

Justification of environmental preferences
The justification of the environmental preference explains which issues have determined the choices made between the various alternatives. For example, when two choices are compared with each other and both score badly on account of energy consumption, then this would not normally be mentioned. We do, however, indicate when one alternative is less degradable than another.

Part 4 lists the main environmental impact of various common materials. Their impact is noted in the justification when specific information about the building component has been given.

19

example

environmental preference

The production process of an aluminium or PVC frame is much more environmentally damaging than that of a wooden frame. Recycled PVC means a substantial fraction has been recycled. Alternatively, future recycling should be guaranteed. Softwood frames are preserved with harmful preservatives as a result of a bad track record. The use of more durable woods is one possible solution.

Untreated softwood frames are also a possible solution provided that the quality of the wood, the specification and finish has received sufficient attention for their durability to be about the same as that of treated frames.

See Part 4 for a more detailed description of the environmental impact of the materials mentioned.

not recommended

The use of non-sustainable wood is not recommended due to the depletion of the ecosystem.

basic selection

Softwood treated with solid borate implant.

comments

The untreated softwood frames mentioned under environmental preference are supplied with a guarantee of 10 years. These frames are however more expensive than the alternatives. The price of frames varies with the area. Aluminium frames are nearly always the most expensive. An advantage of aluminium frames is that an extremely high-grade reuse is possible.

Basic selection

The *Construction* and *Refurbishment* sections each show a *basic selection* for each building element. (This category has been added since the first Dutch edition of the handbook.) The basic selection may not be the preferred alternative from an environmental point of view, but in fact the second or third choice, because the more preferable alternatives may still be more expensive than current solutions or may not be sufficiently proven in practice. The basic selection is a practical solution, having low environmental impact and being easy to implement, without giving rise to practical problems

The basic selection category represents design solutions which have not only been applied in various trials and been technically proven, but which, compared with current alternatives, incur negligible or no additional costs. This product choice should, though, be seen as just a first step within the framework of sustainable building.

This selection can be used immediately as there are no technical problems to overcome and additional costs should also be low.

Availability and costs

Finally, other relevant issues are listed for each building component. In many cases there are stumbling blocks when using less common and less environmentally damaging product alternatives. The cost factor is important: alternatives which are less environmentally harmful often turn out to cost more, which is partly because production is on a small scale, or contractors charge extra because they are not familiar with the product.

In general, the costs quoted here should be regarded as an indication only because experience from previous years has shown that it is impossible to deduce unequivocal cost data – costs depend on the project and region, as well as on the individual contractors and the results of their negotiations. The reproduced cost data are based on information provided in the environmental specification developed by W/E, together with the Architectural Bureau, Inbo.

The preferences and the basic selection are continuously being developed.

There are many places where sustainable building is being applied and this sometimes leads to questions about experiences elsewhere. This handbook intends to fill this need.

7. Examples of projects using EPM

Project 1 Bloemendaal, The Hague

Project information
- Title: Psychiatric Centre Bloemendaal, The Hague
- Type of accommodation: 128 houses for the social sector and 14 for the independent sector
- Amount of accommodation: 142 units
- Project development: Stichting Woningbedrijf Den Haag Centrum
- Investment per unit: average of Dfl. 130,300 total project costs (c. £68,400). Rents vary from Dfl. 370–1,510 (£160–£650) per month
- Architect: Kees van Baalen, Architectenbureau Arpros
- Environmental consultant: Woon/Energie, Gouda
- Year of completion: 1993
- General description: The houses are built for personnel and patients of the psychiatric residence nearby. The houses for the patients are integrated into the site of the psychiatric residence and are designed to allow them to live independently of the main residence.

Sustainable materials

	preference 1	preference 2	preference 3	not recommended
Garden partitioning	**hedges**	•	•	tropical hardwood, preserved wood
Foundation posts	•	**concrete with reclaimed aggregate**	•	concrete without reclaimed aggregate
Ground floor	•	**hollow concrete elements**		solid concrete floor
Insulation, ground floor	**mineral wool**	•	•	•
Upper floor	•	•	**concrete with reclaimed aggregate**	concrete without reclaimed aggregate
Party walls	•	**sand-lime blocks**	•	concrete without reclaimed aggregate
Solid internal walls	•	**flue-gas gypsum**	cellular concrete	•
Internal cavity panelling	•	**sand-lime blocks**	•	concrete
Pitched roof construction	•	**sustainable plywood**	chipboard	•
Pitched roof insulation		**mineral wool**	EPS	
External window frames	**hemlock**	•		tropical hardwood
External doors	**hemlock**	•	•	tropical hardwood
Stairs, internal	**European softwood**	•	•	tropical hardwood
Floor screeds	**flue-gas gypsum anhydrite**	•	•	•
			sand cement	
Internal woodwork	•	**water-based acrylic paint**	•	alkyd paint
External woodwork	•	**high solids alkyd paint**		alkyd paint
Gutters	**none**	•	•	zinc
Drainpipes	**none**	•	•	PVC
Internal waste systems	•	**PP**	•	PVC

bold = actual choice   plain text = project reference

Other measures

A lot of attention has been given to the living environment, as well as to savings of energy and water. Energy-saving measures should reduce the use of natural gas from 2046 m³ to 1435 m³ per year, a reduction of 30%.

The measures taken in order to achieve this were: condensing-boiler, LE-glazing, floor insulation (R=3.5 or U = 0.27) and solar boilers for supplying domestic hot water. Water-saving measures are water-saving taps, toilets and showers. These will reduce water usage by 21%.

Project 2 Ecolonia, Alphen aan de Rijn

Project information
- Title: Ecolonia, Alphen aan de Rijn (Topic 4: integrated life cycle)
- Type of accommodation: four senior houses, and six life cycle houses, two under one roof
- Amount of accommodation: Topic 4; 16
- Project development: Bouwfonds Woningbouw, Delft and Novem, Sittard
- Investment per unit: Dfl. 220,000 (£94,000)
- Architect: Tjerk Reijenga, BEAR Architecten, Gouda
- Environmental consultant: Woon/Energie, Gouda
- Year of completion: 1991–1993
- General description: Ecolonia is a site for new buildings with nine environmental topics, designed by nine different architects. It is a pilot project designed to show that environmentally sound, energy-saving buildings and comfortable living can be combined. Topic 4 is 'extra attention to water-saving and the reuse of building materials'. On a town planning level, strong attention was given to the living environment.

Sustainable materials

	preference 1	preference 2	preference 3	not recommended
External sewers	**ceramic**	•	•	PVC
Foundation posts	•	**concrete with reclaimed aggregate**	•	concrete without reclaimed aggregate
Ground floor	•	**hollow concrete elements**		solid concrete floor
Upper floor	**wooden elements**	•	•	concrete without reclaimed aggregate
	•	•		
Party walls	**timber frame construction**	•	•	concrete without reclaimed aggregate
External wall stairs	**durable wood**	masonry	•	•
Internal wall stairs	**wooden elements**	•	•	concrete
Wall insulation	**cellulose**	•	EPS	•
Pitched roof construction	•	**box panels**	(non-tropical plywood)	•
Pitched roof insulation	**cellulose**	•	EPS	•
External window frames	**untreated softwood**	•	•	tropical hardwood
External wall cladding	**durable wood**	•	synthetic resin bonded	•
Stairs internal	**European softwood**	•	•	tropical hardwood
Floor screed	**flue-gas gypsum anhydrite**	•	sand cement	•
External woodwork	**natural paint**	•	•	alkyd paint
Internal waste systems	•	**PP**	PVC	PVC

bold = actual choice   plain text = project reference

Other measures

Energy saving measures employed in this project are the installation of condensing boilers for low NO_x heating systems (low temperature system), solar boilers for providing domestic hot water, as well as using north-south positioning for the properties and installing double glazing.

A mechanical ventilation system with heat recovery was also installed.

Rainwater is collected in a barrel with a pump, for use in the WC. Other water-saving measures are water-saving toilets, showers and taps. There is also a 'recycling cupboard' a place to collect separated household waste.

Project 3 Westduinen, Kijkduin, The Hague

Project information
- Title: Westduinen in Kijkduin, The Hague
- Type of accommodation: villas
- Amount of accommodation: 39 units
- Project development: Eurowoningen
- Investment per unit: Dfl. 548,000–850,000 (£235,000–363,000)
- Architect: Van Tilburg and Partners, Rotterdam
- Environmental consultant: Woon/Energie, Gouda
- Year of completion: 1995
- General description: the villas are situated in Kijkduin, a seaside resort in The Hague.

Sustainable materials

	preference 1	preference 2	preference 3	not recommended
Building waste	**separate all types**	•	clean rubble, low-grade chemical waste, metal and remainder	•
External sewers	**ceramic**	•	•	•
Upper floors	• •	**ceramic and hollow concrete elements with reclaimed aggregate**	• •	concrete without reclaimed aggregate •
Party walls	•	**sand–lime blocks**	•	concrete without reclaimed aggregate
Solid internal walls	•	**flue-gas gypsum blocks**	cellular concrete	• •
Internal wall stairs	•	**sand–lime blocks**	•	concrete
External wall insulation	•	**mineral wool**	EPS	•
External window frames	•	•	**preserved softwood**	tropical hardwood
External doors	•	**softwood with solid borate implant**	•	tropical hardwood
Internal stairs	**European softwood**	•	•	tropical hardwood
Flat roof covering		**EPDM**	•	•
Internal woodwork	•	•	**blown bitumen**	alkyd paint
External woodwork	•	**high solids alkyd paint**	•	alkyd paint
Internal waste systems	•	**PP**	•	PVC

bold = actual choice   plain text = project reference

Other measures

The energy measures that have been taken are the use of condensing boilers, solar boilers for providing domestic hot water, a large glass surface area on the south-facing external walls, LE-glazing, extra insulation on the ground floors, external walls and roofs. There are also water-saving showers, taps and WCs.

Project 4 Sustainable renovation, Jan Evertsenstraat, Amsterdam

Project information
- Title: complex Jan Evertsenstraat (Hoek Admiralengracht, Amsterdam gordel '20-'40)
- Type of accommodation: 4-room apartments
  Amount of accommodation: 70 apartments and 19 business units
- Building owner: Woningbedrijf, Amsterdam
- Investment per unit: Dfl. 83,598 (£35,725)
- Year of completion: 1926
- Architect in charge of buildings: J.M. van der Mey (Amsterdam School)
- Year of refurbishment: 1993
- Architect in charge of refurbishment: Architectenbureau CASA, Amsterdam
- Environmental consultant: Woon/Energie, Gouda
- Refurbishment entailed: improving the roof and external walls, and renewing living facilities, as well as the actual size of the accommodation to meet certain minimum technical and living standards. Extra insulation and double glazing formed part of the

refurbishment, as well as installing new kitchens, bathrooms, and ceilings. Residents were offered the option of central heating installation. Other measures were glazed verandas on balconies, the installation of combined heating and ventilation systems, green roofs and low-emittance glazing installed in the living room. Expected life extension: 25 years

Sustainable materials

	preference 1	*preference 2*	*preference 3*	*not recommended*
Insulation, cavity wall	•	**mineral wool**	EPS	•
External wall surfacing	**repair of pointing**	•	•	application of synthetic rendering
Cleaning external walls	•	**dry, low pressure**	•	chemical
Sealing external walls	**water-based**	•	•	solvent-based system
Repairing concrete	**mineral filler**	•	•	epoxy-resin filler
Concrete surfacing	**mineral coating**	•	•	other coating
Pitch roof construction	**softwood rafters and battens**	•	chipboard	•
Pitch roof insulation	•	**mineral wool**	EPS	•
External window frames	•		preserved softwood	tropical hardwood
External doors	**durable wood**	•	•	tropical hardwood
External wall cladding	**Western red cedar**	•	synthetic resin bonded	•
Stairs internal	**European softwood**	•	•	tropical hardwood
Flat roof covering		**EPDM**	blown bitumen	•
Fixed coverings	**loose with plants**	•	•	glued
Ceilings	**flue-gas gypsum**	gypsum	•	•
Bathroom and toilet floors	**granite**	tiles	•	•
External woodwork	•	**high solids alkyd paint**	•	alkyd paint
Internal waste systems	•	**PP**	•	PVC

bold = actual choice   plain text = project reference

Other measures

Energy-saving measures used in this project are insulation of the roof and the ground floor, as well as installation of LE-glazing in the front external wall, glazing the veranda on the rear external wall and installation of a central heating system with heat recovery. The front external wall is not insulated because of thermal bridges in the construction. Water-saving WCs were also installed.

Jan Evertsenstraat is a busy shopping street. Noise-reduction measures employed include insulated glass and closed window frames in the front external wall. Indoors the noise was reduced by a false ceiling insulated with mineral wool. Noise-reducing air inlets were not necessary because ventilation was taken from the rear of the property (the air there was cleaner than on the street side of the building). The quality of indoor air is also improved by a closed heating and hot water system instead of an open water heater.

Project 5 'De Straat', Spangen Rotterdam

Project information
- Title: 'De Straat' area, Spangen, Rotterdam
- Type of accommodation: mostly 3 and 4 room flats, but also some 5 and 6 room apartments
- Amount of accommodation: after renovation 122 apartments and 12 business units
- Building owner: Gemeentelijk Woningbedrijf Rotterdam, West district
- Investment per unit: Dfl. 130,732 total project costs (£55,870)
- Year of building completion: 1920
- Year of refurbishment: 1994
- Architect: Akropolis Architecten, Rotterdam
- Environmental consultant: Woon/Energie, Gouda
- Refurbishment entailed: This project had what is known as 'high level renovation', the rear external walls being removed, while the front external walls, load bearing walls and girder systems were not removed. The total number of units was reduced from 212 apartments and 17 business units to 122 apartments and 12 business units.
- Expected life extension: 40 years

Sustainable materials

	preference 1	preference 2	preference 3	not recommended
Privacy screen	•	**deal**	•	tropical hardwood
Upper floor	**Oregon pine underlay**	•	•	tropical plywood
External wall insulation	**cellulose**	mineral wool	•	•
Cleaning external walls	**damp, low pressure**	dry, low pressure	•	•
Sealing external walls	**water–based**	•	•	solvent-based system
Sealing joints	**PE membrane**	•	•	lead
External window frames	**durable wood**	•	•	PVC
External doors	**durable wood**	•	•	tropical hardwood
Stairs, internal	**European softwood**	•	•	tropical hardwood
Balustrades/railings, internal	**European wood**	•	•	tropical hardwood
Flat roof coverings	•	**EPDM**	blown bitumen	•
Fixed coverings	•	•	**mechanical**	glued
External woodwork	•	**high solids alkyd paint**	•	alkyd paint
Gutters	**timber gutter**	•	•	zinc
Gutter lining	**EPDM**	•	•	zinc
Internal waste systems	•	**PP**	•	PVC

bold = actual choice   plain text = project reference

Other measures

Energy-saving measures in this project are HR-glazing and one condensing boiler per unit for heating and hot water, as well as the installation of balanced ventilation with heat recovery. There are also water-saving showers. Noise-reduction measures include the heat recovery equipment, floor insulation, and metal-studded walls and ceilings.

Project 6 Sustainable renovation, Landsherenkwartier, Deventer

Project information
- Title: sustainable renovation 'Landsherenkwartier' in Deventer
- Type of accommodation: 3 and 4 room apartment houses, four storeys each
- Total number: 144
- Building owner: Woningbouwvereiniging VtV
- Investment per unit: Dfl 39,000 (£16,700)
- Year of building completion: 1963
- Year of refurbishment: 1993
- Architect: Sacon, Zwolle
- Environmental consultant: Woon/Energie, Gouda
- Renovation approach: higher living standards were gained by insulating external walls and floors. Repairs were undertaken on the concrete in the construction and on the roof. Window frames, windows and doors were replaced. New kitchens were also installed and bathrooms were refurbished.
- Expected life extension: 20–25 years

Sustainable materials

	preference 1	preference 2	preference 3	not recommended
Concrete repairs	**mineral filler**	•	•	epoxy-resin filler
Concrete surfacing	•	**water-based coating**		other coating
Sealing joints	**PE membrane**	•	•	lead
External window frames	**Oregon pine**	•	•	tropical hardwood
External doors	**hemlock**	•	•	tropical hardwood
Internal waste systems	•	**PP**	•	PVC
Pipe insulation	**cellulose**	•	•	PUR, extruded polystyrene

bold = actual choice   plain text = project reference

26

Other measures
Energy-saving insulation was incorporated into the walls, floors and external walls with panelling. Double glazing and high-efficiency boilers were also installed. Energy-saving measures had to reduce gas usage from 1400 m³ down to 840 m³ a year. Water-saving showers and toilets were also installed, and mechanical ventilation was put into the bathroom.

There were new facilities for separating household waste and attention was given to the living environment by reducing the amount of pavement used, for example, and by creating a community garden.

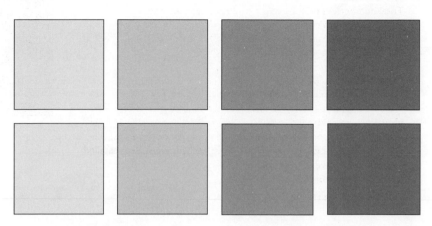

Environmental selection of materials for use in *Construction*

Contents Part 2: Environmental selection of materials for use in *Construction*

Building element			Page
05	**Building site requirements**		
		Building waste	31
06	**Preservative treatments**		
		Wood preservation	32
		Localised preservation (solid implants)	32
		Overall preservation	33
12	**Ground coverings**		
		Ground under suspended floors	34
14	**External sewers and drainage**		
		External sewers	35
15	**Hard landscaping**		
		Hard paving	36
		Semi-hard paving	36
17	**Landscaping and laying out gardens**		
		Garden partitioning	38
		Privacy screens	39
		Outside storage	39
20	**Foundation posts and damp-proof courses**		
		Foundation posts	40
21–25	***Shell construction***		
21–25	**Floor construction**		
		Ground floors	41
		Ground floor insulation	41
		Party floors	42
		Balconies	43
21–25	**Internal wall construction**		
		Party walls	44
		Internal walls	45
		Solid internal walls	45
21–25	**External wall construction**		
		External wall skin	47
		Internal wall skin	47
		Wall insulation	48
21–25	**Roof construction**		
		Roof shape	49
		Pitched roof construction	49
		Pitched roof insulation	50
		Flat roof construction	50
		Flat roof insulation	51
		Flashings	52
30	***Window frames and doors***		
30	**External window frames and doors**		
		External window frames	53
		External doors	53
		Window sills	54
30	**Internal window frames and doors**		
		Internal window frames	55
		Internal doors	55
		Internal door thresholds	56
		Window sills	56
31	**Cladding systems**		
		External wall cladding	57
32	**Stairs and balustrades**		
		Internal stairs	58
		External stairs	58
		Internal balustrades/railings	59
		External balustrades/railings	59
33	**Roof coverings**		
		Pitched roof coverings	61

(handwritten note: Low-Emit & Material)

Building waste

preference 1	preference 2	preference 3	not recommended
separate all types	as preference 3 + wood and synthetics	clean rubble, lowgrade chemical waste, metal and remainder	unseparated waste

environmental preference

The separation of building waste, a by-product in the construction of new houses, opens up opportunities for further use. Reuse saves material and reduces dumping and incineration. Primary reuse – where the material is used again following negligible or no further treatment – is preferable, and occurs more often in demolition or refurbishment than in the construction of new houses. Secondary reuse (recycling) where the materials are reprocessed to new materials in a reprocessing plant demands additional transport and energy consumption and results in the release of harmful substances.
Incineration releases many noxious substances. A number of waste categories, such as wood and synthetic materials, generate energy as heat when incinerated. The environmental benefits gained from reuse, however, are substantially greater.

not recommended

Most building waste used to be dumped. It is recommended that dumping is drastically restricted in view of the environmental implications of landfill.

basic selection

The separation of clean rubble, lowgrade chemical waste, metals, wood, synthetics and a residual fraction generally incurs negligible cost. These fractions can be adjusted according to the project's predicted waste flows.

comments

The separation of waste on site is generally preferable because it is best to tackle problems at their source. Some waste processing firms may prefer their consignments unsorted and to separate the waste themselves. This form of separating waste is appropriate for inner-city locations where space is at a premium, but the disadvantage with it is that building site personnel are not directly involved.

The diagram below describes the principal reprocessing options for each type of waste.
The alternative with the lowest number is practically feasible and this is the preferred choice from an environmental point of view.

31

waste fractions / processing method	primary reuse	secondary reuse	incineration	landfill
rubble	1	2		3
reinforced concrete		1		2
wood	1	2	3	4
synthetics		1	2	3
metals	1	2	3	4
paper and cardboard		1	2	3
glass	1	2		3
(small) chemical waste		1	2	3
other (e.g. domestic waste)		1	2	3

Wood preservation

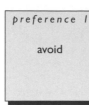  

preference 1 — avoid

preference 2 — localised

preference 3 — overall

not recommended — —

environmental preference

Wood needs to be preserved when there is a threat of decay. (Note: insect damage is not a general problem in the Netherlands, and is therefore not yet considered as a factor in this environmental assessment.) Preservation can often be completely dispensed with, provided that the building element is well specified, a high-quality durable wood (properly seasoned and without knots) is used and that a protective finish is applied and well maintained.

A localised wood preservative in the form of a solid implant is preferred in some cases. Solid implants are inserted into the corner joints of window and door frames, for instance, as these are the most vulnerable locations. Expert opinion as to the efficiency of this measure varies considerably.

Overall preservation of wood is hardly ever necessary, nor is it desirable from an environmental point of view.

32

basic selection

Not given because this depends on the situation. See the respective building elements.

Localised preservation (solid implants)

preference 1 — borates

preference 2 — —

preference 3 — —

not recommended — bifluoride, TBTO

environmental preference

A solid implant, based on borates, has been on the market for some time. This implant is only minimally harmful, degrades well and no noxious substances are released when the wood is burnt. Such implants have the additional advantage that preservation is localised, and as this is a dry implant, the active substances are only released when the degree of moisture reaches 20%, which reduces leaching. The pill remains effective for 5–10 years.

not recommended

Both the dry bifluoride (BF) implant and the liquid pill, based on TBTO (tributyl tin oxide), contain substances which are relatively toxic to the environment.

basic selection

Implants based on borates have been used in many projects and are listed in the basic selection on account of their minimal threat to the environment.

comments

Long-term experience has shown solid implants based on borates to be effective, provided that they contain diffusable preservatives.

Overall preservation

preference 1	preference 2	preference 3	not recommended
borates	quaternary ammonium compounds, zinc soaps, azoles	CCB salts, ZCF salts	CCA salts, improsol (BF) creosote oil

environmental preference

Borates are considerably less harmful to people and the environment than other preservatives. The disadvantage is that they leach in water. While this is not normally an issue, as they are generally in internal or protected situations, it can become a problem where the wood is in contact with the soil (in the case of a garden fence, for example). This can be combated by combining the borates with a natural preservative which renders the wood water-repellent. Natural preservative has no fungicidal effect. If this is not sufficient, then fixed preservatives such as quaternary ammonium compounds, zinc soaps and azoles can be used..

Preservative salts consist of a mixture of mainly heavy metals. CCA (copper chrome arsenic) salts are commonly used salts; their chromium and arsenic content is particularly harmful, though copper, which is responsible for the green colour, is much less harmful. CCB (chromium copper boron) and ZCF (zinc copper fluoride) salts contain fewer harmful elements than the CCA salts. Another important aspect is the ratio of the compounds in the preservative, which to a large extent determines the degree of leaching. Type B CCA salts leach more than type C CCA salts; they are therefore more environmentally damaging.

not recommended

CCA salts are not recommended on account of the presence of chromium and arsenic. Other harmful and poorly degradable preservatives are creosote oil and preservatives based on fluorides and tin oxide. The *commonly used* improsolates are an example of a preservative based on bifluoride.

basic selection

Quaternary ammonium compounds, zinc soaps and azoles are included in the basic selection but only when overall preservation is required.

comments

It is important for overall preservation to be done by firms holding a suitable quality assurance certificate. This ensures the stipulations on the preservative, the application method (high-pressure vacuum in a closed system) and its use (i.e. in contact with the soil or not) are adhered to.

33

Environmental selection of materials for use in *Construction*

34

**Ground under
suspended floors**

preference 1	preference 2	preference 3	not recommended
shells	foamed concrete, sand	expanded clay granules, PE membrane	PVC membrane

environmental preference

A layer of shells can be used to cover the ground under the suspended floor of a house. Shells are considered a renewable raw material as they are produced by sea organisms. Sand extraction, on the other hand, causes damage to the landscape. Shells and sand are washed, but not processed further and so cause no problems in waste disposal.
The renewable characteristic of shells is, however, threatened by large-scale use.
Per functional unit less foamed concrete is needed than shells, sand or expanded clay granules, and the production of foamed concrete takes less energy than is the case with expanded clay granules. Clay granules are fired at high temperatures, which ensures they are light and have a high energy content. The type of clay used must be free of harmful substances, such as sulphur.
Petroleum is the raw material for polyethylene (PE) and polyvinyl chloride (PVC) and requires many stages of processing, thereby releasing harmful substances. The extraction and transport of petroleum leads to pollution. particularly at sea. PE does not contain chlorine, in contrast to PVC.
See Part 4 for a more detailed description of the impact on the environment from these materials.

not recommended

PVC membranes are not recommended since suitable alternatives are available.

basic selection

Sand is common on cost grounds, but PE sheet membrane is preferable in many projects; for this reason it is included in the basic selection. Expanded clay granules are also included in the basic selection.

comments

It is important that the layer of sand, shells or expanded clay granules is applied sufficiently thickly. The required thickness depends on the precise situation and may be more than 500 mm in the case of sand. A sand or shell layer is not always possible if there is only little space under the suspended floor.
Shells are more expensive than sand. Expanded clay granules also act as reasonable heat insulation, depending on the moisture in the air. Clay granules have a capillary effect, so may require the addition of a water repellent. The moisture-regulating action of the various materials differs considerably.

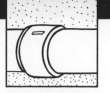

External sewers

preference 1	*preference 2*	*preference 3*	*not recommended*
vitrified clay	PE, PP, concrete	recycled PVC	PVC

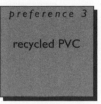

environmental preference

The production process of vitrified clay pipes is considerably cleaner than that of synthetic pipes. These pipes cause few problems for waste disposal.
Polyethylene (PE) and polypropylene (PP) score more favourably on the aspects mentioned than polyvinyl chloride (PVC). Vitrified clay pipes score more favourably than concrete sewers as concrete contains gravel and cement, extraction of which affects the landscape.
Recycled PVC pipes have only a core of secondary material, the internal and external lining is made of primary PVC. These pipes therefore consist of over 50% of secondary PVC. See Part 4 for a more detailed description of the environmental impact of the materials mentioned.

not recommended

The production of PVC and the processing of PVC waste causes problems which are greater than those created in the production of PE and PP. The use of new PVC is therefore not recommended.

basic selection

PE, PP and concrete have been proven to be low-cost (compared with PVC) when applied, and they are therefore included in the basic selection.

comments

The current generation of vitrified clay pipes is suitable for more applications than used to be the case, due to their flexible connections and availability in a range of diameters. Vitrified clay sewer pipes are not available in small diameters and are more expensive on account of the higher labour costs.
Some quality assurance bodies have not yet certified PP external sewers at the time of writing.
Drainage can take place with the aid of sewage pipes made of PE or PVC, or through gravel beds and pits. Drainage pipes are usually lagged with coconut fibre. Polyethylene is also preferred to PVC for drainage pipes. Gravel has the disadvantage that the landscape is affected by extraction. A disadvantage of pipes is that they eventually become silted up. Gravel does not possess this defect.

35

Hard paving

preference 1	preference 2	preference 3	not recommended
recycled concrete slabs	concrete slabs, turf	clay tiles, concrete blocks	asphalt

environmental preference

In general, restricting the extent of paving, and aiming for water-permeable hardening is preferable because it enlarges the water collecting area, which favours the micro-climate. It reduces the burden on the water treatment plant, which helps to prevent annual overflows. Pilot studies already carried out, which have taken this into account, have proven that a reduction of the hardening, including roof surfaces, from about 50% down to 40% is feasible.

Recycled concrete slabs are preferable for paving as they consist, in part, of secondary raw materials. Slabs are generally preferable to clay tiles due to their lower energy content. Grass turf has a limited use because of its structure, but it has the advantage of a smaller amount of material and greater water permeability.

not recommended

The use of asphalt in a residential environment can be avoided. The environmental problems caused by asphalt are the extraction of limestone and gravel, emissions of SO_2, NO_2 and volatile organic compounds (phenols amongst others) in the production and processing, and the release of small amounts of polycyclic aromatic hydrocarbons (PAHs) and asphalt fumes in processing (working conditions).

basic selection

Semi-open pavement is included in the basic selection. The basic choice for continuous paving is recycled concrete slabs because availability is no longer a problem. We expect that the price will no longer remain an obstacle either, in view of the large supply of stone, brick or blockwork waste.

Semi-hard paving

preference 1	preference 2	preference 3	not recommended
wood chippings	sand	shells	gravel

environmental preference

Wood chippings – made by shredding branches and other prunings – are the most appropriate medium for semi-hard paths, but a footpath will need additional new material after about four years. Sand is slightly less desirable, in comparison, because its extraction carries consequences for the landscape and ecosystems. Shells are admittedly a renewable raw material, but the rate of regeneration is too slow for large-scale use.

not recommended

The use of gravel for semi-hard paths is not recommended because the extraction of gravel affects the landscape. There are better, less environmentally-damaging alternatives available for hardening paths.

basic selection   Shells are included in the basic selection for semi-hard paths, but wood chippings are an extremely good alternative; they are easily available and can be used at low cost.

Environmental selection of materials for use in Construction

38

Garden partitioning

preference 1	preference 2	preference 3	not recommended
 hedges	cuttings and pruning waste	untreated wood	recycled PVC, tropical wood, preserved wood

environmental preference

The use of hedges as garden partitioning contributes positively to the living environment. The urban micro-climate (moisture control) is improved and nesting opportunities for various types of animals are increased. Many native shrubs are suitable for this purpose, depending on the soil. Some well-known examples are privet or hornbeam, blackthorn and hawthorn.

Partitions of cuttings and pruning waste consist of wood thinnings which have been woven. The thinnings are a waste product and put to good use in this way. It is debatable whether a partition of untreated softwood posts is a good idea because experience shows that many occupants remove and replace the existing partitioning when laying out a garden.

not recommended

The use of non-sustainable wood is not recommended, due to the effects on the ecosystem. Treated wood is also not recommended on account of the leaching of preservatives. Nor should recycled PVC posts be used. The use of synthetic waste for the production of garden fixtures and fittings is a form of reuse, but an important minus is that it concerns a low-grade application. The use of such products is really dumping in disguise. PVC is stored, albeit usefully, before it actually ends up as landfill or in the incinerator. Uncertainty with regard to the life-span due to the laying out of gardens also plays a part. The risk of premature dumping or incineration is great.
If posts are used for fencing then the omission of steel wires should be considered. They can also harm the environment because of their heavy galvanisation and their short life-span. Hemp rope should be considered if such a form of demarcation is desired.

basic selection

Untreated softwood posts, possibly combined with hemp rope, are cheaper and usually functional.

Privacy screens

preference 1	*preference 2*	*preference 3*	*not recommended*
hedges	sustainable durable wood	masonry	tropical wood, preserved wood

environmental preference

See *garden partitioning* for preference 1. A privacy screen is normally expected to last longer than garden partitioning. We have therefore ranked durable wood and masonry as second and third choices. Masonry is more or less harmful to the environment depending on which block type is used.
See Part 4 for a more detailed description of the environmental impact of the materials mentioned.

not recommended

See *garden partitioning*.

basic selection

A masonry privacy screen is included in the basic selection; it is more expensive than the alternatives. The first and second preferences are cheaper.

comments

A wooden privacy screen should be prevented from coming into contact with damp soil by providing the posts with a concrete footing.

Outside storage

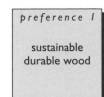

preference 1	*preference 2*	*preference 3*	*not recommended*
sustainable durable wood	painted softwood	masonry, prefabricated concrete	tropical wood, preserved wood

environmental preference

Such an application demands a long life-span, which is why hardwood is preferred unless it is to be painted.
A painted shed made of softwood has the disadvantage that it must be painted regularly during its lifetime. Boiled paint (see Part 4) is preferable to conventional paints for this application, as the paint is less harmful and a lower quantity is required. It can be applied less frequently.
An external shed of masonry or prefab concrete is more environmentally damaging on account of the quantity and the type of raw materials used, but it has the advantage of a longer life-span. The prefab concrete shed is also simple to dismantle and reassemble.
See Part 4 for a more detailed description of the environmental impact of the materials mentioned.

not recommended

See *garden partitioning*.

basic selection

An external shed of masonry or prefabricated concrete is included in the basic selection. A prefabricated shed is no more expensive than one made of treated wood. A masonry shed is dearer, however.

comments

The preference given in 21–25 *roof shape* also applies to the roof of the shed.

Foundation posts

preference 1	*preference 2*	*preference 3*	*not recommended*
wood with top	concrete with reclaimed aggregate	—	concrete without reclaimed aggregate

environmental preference

A wooden foundation post is the top preference as the material is renewable. Wooden posts must have a concrete top. A square pre-stressed concrete top is now on the market, which saves about 50% of raw materials compared with a traditional round top. The use of reclaimed aggregate (from demolition waste) in concrete foundation posts – a common practice in the Netherlands – would also limit the quantity of new gravel required.
See Part 4 for a more detailed description of the environmental impact of the materials mentioned.

not recommended

The use of concrete without incorporating reclaimed aggregate from demolition waste is not recommended due to problems pertaining to the extraction of gravel. The availability of reclaimed aggregate concrete is still limited in some areas. However, this is expected to change soon.

basic selection

There is, at present, still a limited number of suppliers for foundation posts with reclaimed aggregate. Nevertheless the price is comparable with that of the standard concrete post, so that the reclaimed aggregate post is included in the basic selection.

comments

Wooden posts are suitable in many cases. The maximum length and the loadbearing strength, however, are limiting factors.

40

21–25 Floor construction

For floor screeds see 42

Ground floors

preference 1	*preference 2*	*preference 3*	*not recommended*
hollow ceramic elements	hollow concrete elements with reclaimed aggregate or limestone	solid concrete with reclaimed aggregate or limestone	solid concrete without replacement for gravel

environmental preference

Tiled floors and floors made of hollow concrete elements demand less material and use less energy than a solid concrete floor. With concrete elements a high saving (50%) can also be made on the use of steel reinforcement. One advantage of ceramic elements is that the raw materials required are more common than those needed for concrete elements. The use of reclaimed aggregate (from demolition waste) or limestone as a substitute for gravel lessens the depletion of the gravel supply and the effects on the landscape that gravel extraction causes. The use of reclaimed aggregate together with hollow concrete elements is, however, hardly possible. Optimising the quantity of material is preferable to the use of reclaimed aggregate.
See Part 4 for a more detailed description of the impact on the environment of the materials mentioned.

not recommended

Concrete has the disadvantage that the raw materials needed are scarce. A solid concrete floor is not recommended because suitable alternatives are available.

basic selection

Hollow concrete elements. The large-scale availability of concrete elements with reclaimed aggregate and ceramic elements is still problematic.

comments

A wooden floor is less environmentally damaging in the use of materials than the alternatives mentioned. However, it is questionable whether an airtight seal could be created, even with additional measures such as incorporating a suspended sub-floor. Wood used in such a location would also be vulnerable to fungal attacks. A high degree of moisture and the presence of the remains of building materials contribute greatly to this.
A wooden ground floor has therefore been excluded from the environmental preference for the construction of new dwellings. If a suitable technical solution is found, then a wooden floor would be the preferred choice.

Ground floor insulation

preference 1	*preference 2*	*preference 3*	*not recommended*
mineral wool, EPS	foamed glass	perlite	extruded polystyrene, PUR

environmental preference

The production process of mineral wool and expanded polystyrene (EPS) requires less energy and results in a smaller emission of noxious substances than the production process of the skin and mucous membranes must be protected against foamed glass and

perlite. The fibres which can cause irritation when mineral wool is used.
See Part 4 for a more detailed description of the environmental effects of the materials mentioned.

not recommended

Polyurethane (PUR) and extruded polystyrene are considerably more harmful to the environment than mineral wool. The use of (H)CFCs as foaming agents for extruded polystyrene and PUR should be avoided because of the damage caused to the ozone layer.

basic selection

Mineral wool and EPS is included in the basic selection as it is easily available without additional costs, even when used in combination with prefabricated flooring elements.

comments

The insulation layer must meet certain requirements in its compressibility because of its prefabricated stone flooring elements. With mineral wool this means that a special 'hard-pressed' variety is required.
Attention must be paid to how the insulation layer is fixed to the concrete elements. Cassette rib concrete flooring elements have recently come onto the market, with an insulating layer of mineral wool; their insulation rating is higher and their cost comparable to EPS.

Party floors

preference 1	*preference 2*	*preference 3*	*not recommended*
wooden elements	hollow ceramic and concrete elements with reclaimed aggregate	concrete with reclaimed aggregate	concrete without reclaimed aggregate

environmental preference

Wood is a renewable material, whereas the raw materials required for concrete are scarce and their extraction affects the landscape. A wooden floor also requires less material than a stone one, and causes less problems for waste disposal than a concrete floor.
See Part 4 for a more detailed description of the environmental impact of the materials mentioned.

not recommended

The use of concrete without reclaimed aggregate is not recommended as less environmentally-damaging alternatives are available.

basic selection

Concrete with reclaimed aggregate in broad slab flooring, e.g. is included in the basic selection. The availability of reclaimed aggregate concrete varies depending on the area.

comments

The use of a wooden upper floor requires extra consideration in the specification with regard to sound insulation. A floating floor and/or a suspended false ceiling is desirable. The availability of ceramic and hollow concrete elements with reclaimed aggregate is at present unproblematic.

Balconies

preference 1	preference 2	preference 3	not recommended
sustainable durable wood elements	sectional steel, aluminium	prefabricated concrete with reclaimed aggregate	concrete without rubble, tropical wood

environmental preference

Balconies are generally badly affected by moisture, which demands the use of a durable material. Wood with a Class II durability rating does not need to be treated when used externally. Wood is a renewable material and degrades well in the decomposition phase. Sectional steel and aluminium elements can be reused at a later stage, but steel must be treated to prevent corrosion. The extraction and production of aluminium is harmful to the environment, particularly because its high energy content. Aluminium, like steel, is eminently reusable.

Prefabricated concrete with reclaimed aggregate is not as favourable as the alternatives mentioned above with regard to the raw materials used, but it is an obvious choice for use in combination with a concrete support structure. The life-span is estimated to be greater than that of other alternatives. Prefabricated concrete is preferable to concrete cast on site because the factory uses less material and causes less pollution.

See Part 4 for a more detailed description of the environmental impact of the materials mentioned.

not recommended

The use of non-sustainable wood is not recommended due to the impact on the ecosystem. The use of concrete without reclaimed aggregate is also not recommended due to the problems relating to gravel extraction.

basic selection

Prefabricated concrete with reclaimed aggregate. The availability of this may still be problematic depending on the area.

comments

A wooden balcony can be used in many cases, but is less in line with present building practice than the use of reclaimed aggregate concrete. As a result, the price of a wooden balcony is therefore considerably higher than that of a prefabricated concrete element.

43

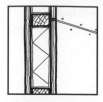

21–25 Internal wall construction

For non-solid internal walls see 44

Party walls

preference 1	*preference 2*	*preference 3*	*not recommended*
loam construction, timber frame construction	sand-lime-blocks, cellular concrete blocks	porous brick, concrete with reclaimed aggregate, limestone	solid concrete without a substitute for gravel

environmental preference

Wood is a renewable material and is less environmentally damaging than the alternatives. European softwood is used for timber frame construction. Components such as plasterboard and mineral wool are, like the timber frame, reasonably environmentally friendly. Mineral wool has the property of being fire-resistant, as well as offering acoustic and thermal insulation. The use of timber in frame construction means that less material is needed than would be the case for solid concrete walls. The lightweight support construction has a positive effect in that a lighter foundation structure is needed. Loam is readily available and its extraction has minimal effect on the environment. Its production and transport damage the environment only to a small degree.

Sand-lime-brick has the advantage that the raw materials used are less scarce and the extraction affects the landscape less than concrete and concrete with reclaimed aggregate. Its production also requires little energy and the process is relatively pollution-free. Cellular concrete is less heavy and thus saves on material use.

Porous brick on the other hand has a high energy content but has the advantage that the raw materials (clay and sawdust) are less environmentally damaging. As the sawdust burns up when the brick is fired, a light brick with cavities is created.

See Part 4 for a more detailed description of the environmental impact of the materials mentioned

not recommended

The use of concrete without reclaimed aggregate is not recommended, as other, less environmentally damaging alternatives are available. .

basic selection

Concrete with reclaimed aggregate and porous brick. This product is not easily available in some areas. Sand-lime-brick and cellular concrete are preferable to concrete with reclaimed aggregate on account of the reduced threat to the environment and the broad range of its applications. Often there is no increase in cost.

comments

Timber frame construction has disadvantages, as well as environmental advantages. It contains less mass so that extra consideration should be given to insulation with regard to the transmission of airborne sound. Special plugs must be used for fixing heavy objects to cavity walls. The vulnerability of the finish to mechanical stress varies depending on the type of skin used.

Sound insulation should also be considered when concrete materials are used.

A non-anchored cavity wall construction is preferable for all concrete variants. The cavity should start at least 500 mm below the ground floor and extend to the roof in order to be effective. Porous brick has the disadvantage that the maximum available format is considerably smaller than that of, say, sand-lime-blocks. As a result its use is much more labour-intensive with consequently higher costs.

Sand-lime-blocks are used with a block clamp. A special block clamp has been developed for cementing a diaphragm cavity wall, which reduces the additional costs of such a cavity wall (120–40–120 mm) compared with a solid version (300 mm). It is also possible in principle to use a loam construction for the support structure.

44

Internal walls

preference 1	preference 2	preference 3	not recommended
frames and panels	solid	—	—

environmental preference

An internal wall consisting of a frame with panels has the advantage that less material is needed than for solid walls. A cavity wall is also relatively simple to remove. Less waste is produced if the layout of the house is changed.
As a building method it links in very well with a support structure based on a timber frame construction. A choice of solid, concrete interior walls is more obvious for concrete construction methods.

basic selection

No basic selection is included as this depends on the method of building and the functional demands being made.

comments

An internal wall consisting of a frame with panels has little mass and therefore minimal sound insulation. This is the case for enclosed dwellings, as well as for terraced and town houses.
Attaching objects to internal cavity walls is less simple for the occupants. Special plugs must be used.

Solid internal walls

preference 1	preference 2	preference 3	not recommended
loam construction	flue-gas gypsum blocks, sand-lime blocks	cellular concrete blocks, natural gypsum blocks	prefabricated concrete

environmental preference

Loam consists of a mixture of clay, sand and possibly straw. Loam construction is unusual on account of its labour-intensive character, but it has many environmental advantages: it consumes no scarce raw materials, the production process is not harmful and it has a very low energy content.
An internal wall of sand-lime blocks has the advantage that the raw material, sand, is plentiful, production demands little energy and the production process for the blocks is a relatively clean one. Concrete blockwork is made from gypsum, a by-product from electricity power plants, which counts in its favour. Cellular concrete has the disadvantage that the required raw materials are scarce and energy consumption during production is rather high. Natural gypsum scores less well than flue-gas gypsum due to the impact on the landscape caused by its extraction.
See Part 4 for a more detailed description of the environmental impact of the materials mentioned.

not recommended

The use of prefabricated concrete elements for internal walls is not recommended because of the higher environmental load which concrete poses compared with other, extremely suitable and current alternatives. Using prefabricated concrete elements also often involves the use of PUR foam or other sealants.

basic selection

Flue-gas gypsum blocks are now freely available and can be used at low cost.

comments

The junction of solid internal walls to load-bearing walls and ceilings requires special consideration. Gypsum blocks generally involve the use of PVC mouldings which seal the gap visually. This can be avoided by the use of elastic joining-tape and finishing joinery. There is little difference in price between these materials. Producers of natural gypsum blocks and board are in the process of changing over to flue-gas gypsum recovered from electricity power plants instead of natural gypsum. This is attractive in view of the problems with the extraction of natural gypsum, particularly in Germany.

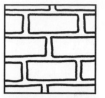

21–25 External wall construction

For external wall insulation and rendering see 40
For external wall cladding see 31

External wall skin

preference 1	preference 2	preference 3	not recommended
sustainable durable wood, loam construction	masonry	fibre cement resin-bonded plywood	tropical wood, preserved softwood

environmental preference

By 'durable wood' we mean an external wall cladding of wooden panels made from durable wood. These wooden elements consist of a renewable and less environmentally damaging material, as long as they remain unpainted and untreated. Loam, a mixture of clay and sand and possibly straw, may not be common in the construction industry as it is so labour-intensive to use/install or to make, but as a building material it has many environmental advantages. External walls made of straw loam must be rendered with a special mortar for example, so as to be made waterproof.
Brickwork is less favourable than loam, due to the energy required to fire the brick, but is preferred to fibre concrete, non tropical plywood and synthetic resin cladding on account of the increased durability and its more or less maintenance-free characteristics. The materials used for external wall cladding are liable to get dirty which makes periodic cleaning desirable.
See Part 4 for a more detailed description of the environmental impact of the materials mentioned.

not recommended

The use of non-sustainable tropical wood is not recommended on account of its effects on ecosystems and the depletion of tropical rain forests. Treated wood is not recommended because of the leaching of preservatives, which can be harmful to the environment.

basic selection

Brickwork is already used on a large scale and is included in the basic selection.

comments

Woodwork as external wall cladding material can be protected with boiled paint. This is less environmentally-damaging paint which lasts between 10 and 30 years.

47

Internal wall skin

preference 1	preference 2	preference 3	not recommended
wooden elements, loam construction	sand-lime blocks, flue-gas gypsum blocks	cellular concrete, blocks, natural gypsum blocks	concrete

environmental preference

European softwood is used for the framework of wooden wall panels. Wood is a renewable material and is therefore less environmentally-damaging. Other components of wood-frame construction types, such as plasterboard and mineral wool, also pose a reduced threat to the environment.
Mineral wool has the quality of being fire-resistant, as well as offering acoustic and thermal insulation. Timber frame construction uses less material than solid concrete walls. The total thickness of the wall can remain limited, even with a high degree of

insulation, as the insulation is placed inside the framework. See *external wall skin* for considerations with regard to loam construction.

Sand-lime blocks and plasterboard are preferable to other stone-like materials on account of the relatively favourable composition. Sand-lime-blocks consist almost completely of sand, and plasterboard is made from a by-product. See Part 4 for a more detailed description of the environmental impact of the materials mentioned.

not recommended

The use of concrete is not recommended as sufficient alternatives are available which are less threatening to the environment.

basic selection

Sand-lime block is included in the basic selection: it is relatively cheap and is common in concrete construction methods. Wall panels made of prefabricated wooden wall filling elements are quite suitable in most cases; these are even less environmentally damaging.

comments

Consideration should be given to junctions with load-bearing walls when using external wall filling elements. The use of polyurethane foam can be eliminated with a good specification and attention to sizing.

Wooden wall panels are about 10% more expensive than sand-lime blocks, but the total thickness of the facade structure is however about 50 mm less, which gives a considerable saving in materials for partitioning wall and roof at a similar house depth.

Wall insulation

preference 1	*preference 2*	*preference 3*	*not recommended*
cork, cellulose	mineral wool	EPS, foamed glass	PUR, extruded polystyrene

48

environmental preference

Cork and cellulose have the advantage that the raw materials are renewable, their production uses little energy and is relatively clean, and the waste is easily degradable. Cellulose is made of the by-product of waste paper. Cellulose can be used in properly enclosed constructions, such as a prefabricated wooden wall element. Application in the cavity is not possible. More energy is required for the production of mineral wool and the degradability of the material is also bad. Skin and mucous membranes must be protected against mineral wool fibres which can cause irritation when working with this material.

The impact of expanded polystyrene (EPS) on the environment is greater than that of the use of mineral wool, from the extraction of petroleum, via the refining process, up to and including the processing of waste. The environmental effects of foamed glass are comparable to those of EPS. The material is used particularly for insulation in an external wall insulation system.

In this case we recommend that the use of bitumen be avoided as a means of fixing.

not recommended

Polyurethane (PUR) and extruded polystyrene threaten the environment more than mineral wool. Damage to the ozone layer inhibits the use of (H)CFCs as a foaming agent. See Part 4 for a more detailed description of the environmental impact of the materials mentioned.

basic selection

Mineral wool is included in the basic selection on account of its suitability and current application. Foamed glass is much more expensive than mineral wool.

comments

Consideration should be given to preventing material from sagging, which could result in large gaps and cold bridges, when using mineral wool sheets as cavity insulation. A possible solution would be to support the insulation with wires stretched crosswise in the structure.

21–25 Roof construction

For roof coverings see 33

Roof shape

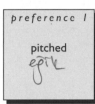

preference 1	preference 2	preference 3	not recommended
pitched	arched	flat	—

environmental preference

The advantage of pitched and arched roofs is that rainwater flows off easily, reducing the demands on waterproofing. The covering on a flat roof, however, must be completely waterproof. Experience also shows that rainwater regularly remains on flat roofs which taxes the covering. The covering of a roof with arches needs to be flexible.
Flat, as well as arched roofs require a roofing material which poses rather a large threat to the environment. A pitched roof therefore is preferred.
Concrete and clay tiles used as roof coverings for a pitched roof are less environmentally damaging than the EPDM membrane mentioned as a first choice for a flat roof.
See Part 4 for a more detailed description of the environmental impact of the materials mentioned.

basic selection

It is not desirable to include this element in a basic selection for aesthetic reasons.

comments

Ventilation is more difficult with both flat and arched roofs on account of the lack of openings, which may cause condensation and damp problems.

49

Pitched roof construction

preference 1	preference 2	preference 3	not recommended
sustainable wood	box panels, sustainable plywood, chipboard (<2mg formaldehyde)	chipboard	plywood made from tropical wood

environmental preference

A traditional roof construction of softwood purlins with softwood joinery is preferable. Softwood joinery does not contain environmentally damaging adhesives, in contrast to plywood.
The box panels in common use are fast to work with on site and have the environmental advantage that it is possible to use cellulose insulation.
It must however be a box with an OSB finish or a plywood finish which is not made of tropical woods, such as Oregon pine. A new type of chipboard with less than 2 mg of formaldehyde per kg has recently been developed.
Roof elements with an insulation layer glued to the panels have the disadvantage that the various components can barely be separated after demolition. A loose or mechanically fixed insulation layer is therefore preferable in all cases.
See Part 4 for a more detailed description of the environmental impact of the materials mentioned.

not recommended

Plywood boards made from tropical wood are not recommended on account of the depletion of tropical rain forests.

basic selection

Roof panelling made from plywood boards containing non-tropical woods, e.g. Oregon pine, is included in the basic selection. It is already a much-used product in current construction practice.

comments

The fixing of softwood joinery is more labour-intensive, which makes the cost higher than for sheet materials. A box panel (with a filling of mineral wool) is 10%–20% cheaper than the other variants. A filling of cellulose, on the other hand, is a little more expensive.

Pitched roof insulation

preference 1	preference 2	preference 3	not recommended
cork, cellulose, sheep's wool	mineral wool	EPS	PUR, extruded polystyrene

environmental preference

Cork, sheep's wool and cellulose have the advantage that the raw materials are renewable, that the production demands little energy and is relatively clean, and that the waste is degradable. Cellulose is made of old paper.
More energy is required for the production of mineral wool, and its degradability is poor. Also, skin and mucous membranes must be protected against wool fibres which can cause irritation when working with this material.
Expanded polystyrene (EPS) poses a greater threat to the environment than the use of mineral wool, from the extraction of petroleum, via the refining process, up to and including processing of the waste.

not recommended

Polyurethane (PUR) and extruded polystyrene threaten the environment considerably more than mineral wool. Damage to the ozone layer inhibits the use of (H)CFCs as foaming agents for extruded polystyrene and PUR.
See Part 4 for a more detailed description of the environmental impact of the materials mentioned.

basic selection

Mineral wool is included in the basic selection on account of its suitability and current application.

comments

Cellulose can in principle only be used in situations where moisture is not a problem, that is for sloping roofs in closed box panels. The large-scale availability of cork is not guaranteed and costs are also considerably higher than for alternatives.

Flat roof construction

preference 1	preference 2	preference 3	not recommended
softwood rafters and roof coverings	steel sheets, cellular concrete	concrete with reclaimed aggregate	concrete without reclaimed aggregate

environmental preference

A traditional roof construction of softwood rafters with softwood joinery is also preferable for flat roofs. Softwood panels do not contain environmentally harmful adhesives, in contrast to plywood.

Profiled steel plates can be used for flat roofs, stretching from load-bearing wall to load-bearing wall, without any support structures below. The steel plate is extremely thin (e.g. 0.88 mm) which limits the amount of material used. A disadvantage is the galvanised thermal layer which is essential for prevention of corrosion.
Glass-reinforced concrete contains less scarce raw materials in comparison with 'normal' concrete. To a lesser extent this is also the case for concrete with 20% reclaimed aggregate as a gravel substitute. By using hollow elements one can save on concrete.
See Part 4 for a more detailed description of the environmental impact of the materials mentioned.

not recommended

The use of concrete without reclaimed aggregate is not recommended in view of the large amounts of gravel and cement which are used for this application.
Plywood sheets made from tropical hardwood should be avoided due to the depletion of tropical rain forests.

basic selection

Concrete with reclaimed aggregate is included in the basic selection. Availability may be problematic however.

comments

The fitting of softwood joinery is more labour-intensive, which makes the cost higher than that of alternatives.

Flat roof insulation

preference 1	*preference 2*	*preference 3*	*not recommended*
cork	EPS, mineral wool, foamed glass	perlite	PUR, extruded polystyrene

environmental preference

Cork has the advantage that it is a renewable raw material, the extraction costs little energy and is relatively clean, and the waste is degradable. Mineral wool must stand up to being walked on when used as insulation material for a warm roof, which means that so-called hard-pressed sheets must be used. The production of hard-pressed mineral wool demands more energy than the 'normal' sheets.
The degradability of mineral wool is poor. Skin and mucous membranes must be protected against wool fibres which can cause irritation when working with this material.
Foamed glass and expanded polystyrene (EPS) pose threats to the environment similar to those from the use of mineral wool due to the high density of mineral wool needed.
See Part 4 for a more detailed description of the environmental impact of the materials mentioned.

not recommended

Extruded polystyrene and polyurethane (PUR) cause pollution which is considerably greater than that caused by mineral wool and EPS. The use of (H)CFCs as foaming agents for extruded polystyrene and PUR is not recommended on account of the damage to the ozone layer.

basic selection

Mineral wool sheets are included in the basic selection as this material is used regularly for this application.

comments

With all insulation materials the method of fixing is paramount for future reuse of the building elements at a later stage. Large-scale availability of cork is not guaranteed.

Flashings

preference 1 PE membrane, EPDM membrane PIB (with aluminium gas)	*preference 2* —	*preference 3* —	*not recommended* lead, zinc

environmental preference

Polyethylene (PE) and ethylene-propylene diene monomer (EPDM) membranes are more durable than zinc. PE, EPDM, bitumen and polyisobutene (PIB) are less harmful and more readily available alternatives to lead and zinc.
See Part 4 for a more detailed description of the environmental impact of the materials mentioned.

not recommended

Lead is extremely harmful to human health. Lead enters the environment during its use as lead flashings and later during the decomposition stage.
Used zinc is not recommended as corrosion can lead to the contamination of wastewater or soil with consequent damage to many organisms. Zinc is also a scarce resource with a relatively short life.

basic selection

PE and EPDM membranes can be used around frames and for filling internal cavity wall panels. As the use of lead cannot be avoided in all cases we have not included this unit in the basic selection.

comments

When PE and EPDM membranes are used for the junction then these membranes must be prevented from blowing off in the wind. The use of lead proves to be inevitable in certain situations, such as at the junction of a tiled roof with rising brickwork. These membranes are about 20% more expensive than zinc and lead.

52

30 External window frames and doors

For preservative treatment see 06
For glazing see 34
For paintwork see 46

External window frames

preference 1	preference 2	preference 3	not recommended
sustainable, durable wood, untreated softwood	softwood with solid borate implant	aluminium, preserved softwood, recycled PVC	tropical wood, PVC

environmental preference

The production process of an aluminium or PVC frame is much more environmentally damaging than that of a wooden frame. 'Recycled PVC' means a substantial fraction has been recycled. Alternatively, future recycling should be guaranteed. Poor quality softwood, requiring large amounts of preservative, was much used in the 1960s and 70s, and softwood gained a poor reputation. Today, though softwood frames are often of high quality, the practice of using large amounts of preservative remains, resulting in much 'over' preserved softwood. The use of more durable woods is one possible solution. Untreated softwood frames are also a possible solution, provided that the quality of the selected wood, the specification and finish has received sufficient attention for their durability to be about the same as that of treated frames.
See Part 4 for a more detailed description of the environmental impact of the materials mentioned.

not recommended

Use of non-sustainable wood is not recommended due to the depletion of the ecosystem.

basic selection

Softwood treated with solid borate implants.

comments

The untreated softwood frames mentioned under environmental preference are supplied with a guarantee of 10 years. These frames are however more expensive than the alternatives. The price of frames varies with the area. Aluminium frames are nearly always the most expensive. An advantage of aluminium frames is that an extremely high-grade reuse is possible.

External doors

preference 1	preference 2	preference 3	not recommended
sustainable durable wood, untreated softwood	softwood with solid borate implant, sustainable plywood	aluminium, preserved softwood, recycled PVC	tropical wood, PVC

environmental preference

Wooden external doors may be treated with harmful preservatives in order to prevent wood decay when damp is a factor needing to be considered. Durable woods are less environmentally damaging than the alternatives.
Untreated softwood doors, in which the quality of the wood, the specification and the finish have been carefully safeguarded, are also satisfactory. A plywood door is also a possible alternative, but its disadvantage lies in the use of adhesives which can be harmful to the environment.
The production process for a wooden external door is much less environmentally damaging than that of an aluminium or PVC external door. One advantage of aluminium doors over PVC is the possibility of high-grade recycling. 'Recycled PVC' means a substantial fraction has been recycled. Alternatively, future recycling should be guaranteed.

53

Balcony and access doors are often protected against damp by respectively overhanging balconies or galleries and entrances or awnings. Untreated pine or deal doors can be used satisfactorily here.
See Part 4 for a more detailed description of the environmental impact of the materials mentioned.

not recommended

The use of non-sustainable wood is not recommended on account of the effects on the ecosystem. Plywood should not be made of tropical wood.

basic selection

An external door made of plywood or softwood, possibly with a solid implant based on borates, is included in the basic selection as these are common types of doors.

Window sills

preference 1	*preference 2*	*preference 3*	*not recommended*
ceramic masonry, solid natural stone	prefabricated concrete, manufactured stone	synthetic stone, aluminium, fibre concrete	—

environmental preference

The production processes of aluminium, synthetic stone, manufactured (cast) stone and prefabricated concrete sills cause more pollution than production of ceramic or solid natural stone sills.
The durability of ceramic, natural stone or concrete sills is also greater. Prefabricated concrete is the second choice due to the use of gravel, which is scarce. The disadvantage of manufactured stone is the use of harmful bonding substances.
See Part 4 for a more detailed description of the environmental impact of the materials mentioned.

basic selection

We have included sills of synthetic stone, aluminium and fibre concrete sheet material in the basic selection because preferences 1 and 2 cannot be used in combination with external wall cladding.

54

30 Internal window frames and doors

For glazing see 34
For paintwork see 46

Internal window frames

preference 1	*preference 2*	*preference 3*	*not recommended*
sustainable wood	galvanised and coated steel	—	tropical wood

environmental preference
The production process of a steel frame is more environmentally damaging than that of a softwood frame. Wooden frames are preferred despite the larger quantity of material used.
See Part 4 for a more detailed description of the environmental impact of the materials mentioned.

not recommended
The use of non-sustainable wood is not recommended on account of the depletion of the ecosystems.

basic selection
Softwood internal frames.

comments
Softwood internal frames are usually slightly cheaper than steel frames, but the difference in cost depends on the method of construction.

Internal doors

preference 1	*preference 2*	*preference 3*	*not recommended*
honeycomb with hardboard skins	European softwood	sustainable plywood, chipboard	tropical wood

environmental preference
Plywood pollutes more than softwood. The amount of material needed for a honeycomb door with a hardboard skin is much smaller, and this is the reason for a door from such material being considered preferable. The production process of an aluminium or steel door causes considerably more pollution than that of an untreated softwood internal door. The plywood internal doors are faced with a synthetic layer (melamine) which impedes a sound processing of waste.
See Part 4 for a more detailed description of the environmental impact of the materials mentioned.

not recommended
The use of non-sustainable wood is not recommended on account of the depletion of ecosystem.

basic selection
Honeycomb door with hardboard skins.

comments
The honeycomb door with hardboard skins is the cheapest.

Internal door thresholds

environmental preference

The production process of steel thresholds is considerably more harmful to the environment than that of wooden thresholds. Hardwoods are preferable as they stand up better against wear and tear. Thresholds made from European deciduous trees have a longer life-span than thresholds made of softwood.
See Part 4 for a more detailed description of the environmental impact of the materials mentioned.

not recommended

The use of non-sustainable hardwood is not recommended on account of the depletion of the ecosystem.

basic selection

Sustainable durable wood. In particular thresholds made of beech are already widely used, except in wet environments.

Window sills

environmental preference

The production process of fibre cement, chipboard and synthetic stone window sills causes worse pollution than that of the stone-like materials and of wood. An asset of wood (also raw material for plywood) is that it is a renewable raw material. A wooden window sill still requires surface treatment.
Chipboard and synthetic stone have a larger amount of harmful adhesives than plywood or manufactured (cast) stone. The adhesives can cause problems during production, during occupation and as waste material. Synthetic stone is more polluting than manufactured stone, due to the use of bonding agents. Chipboard window sills are faced with a synthetic layer (melamine) which complicates sound waste processing.
See Part 4 for a more detailed description of the environmental impact of the materials mentioned.

basic selection

Sustainable plywood.

comments

Tiles are less suitable than wood in certain situations, e.g. in the case of a wooden wall panel. A window sill made of tiles is the cheapest, followed by a window sill made of chipboard or solid softwood. Solid softwood, however, requires more maintenance.

**External wall
cladding**

preference 1	preference 2	preference 3	not recommended
sustainable durable wood	sustainable plywood, synthetic resin-bonded (wood-fibre) board	fibre cement, synthetic resin bonded (paper) board	tropical wood, steel

environmental preference

Wood is renewable and degrades easily, an advantage over fibre cement and synthetic resin board. Wood preservation and paintwork can be dispensed with if durable woods are used. This causes less pollution and requires less maintenance during occupation. The objection to plywood and synthetic resin board lies in the bonding agents used (synthetic resins), the production of which harms the environment. The percentage of bonding agents in synthetic resin boards is, at about 30%, higher than in plywood, which is at about 5%, and additional energy is required for its production. The harm to the environment resulting from maintenance (varnish, paint) and the quality and quantity of wood required for the veneers puts plywood at a disadvantage. Wood produced from thinning, remnants and recycled sheet material, can be used for synthetic resin board based on wood fibres, but only paper can be used in the production of synthetic resin board based on paper laminate. Using recycled board material is not an option.
Cement is the bonding agent used in fibre cement board. It has the drawback that the raw materials are scarce. Its other drawbacks, compared with other boards, are increased weight per square metre and greater vulnerability.
See Part 4 for a more detailed description of the environmental impact of the materials mentioned.

not recommended

The use of non-sustainable wood is not recommended on account of the depletion of the ecosystem.
The extraction of coal (coke) and iron ore for steel and the production of steel results in considerable damage to the environment. Steel has been put in the 'not recommended' category because sufficient alternatives are available.

basic selection

Fibre cement and synthetic resin bonded sheets are included in the basic selection.

comments

Untreated durable woods become grey over the years because they are affected by the weather. The greying has no deleterious effect on the quality of the wood. Cladding with durable wood or plywood is the cheapest solution, but plywood must be regularly maintained. The cost of synthetic fibre bonded sheets is highest; however, they have the advantage of requiring hardly any maintenance.

57

Internal stairs

preference 1 European wood	*preference 2* steel	*preference 3* concrete with reclaimed aggregate	*not recommended* tropical wood

environmental preference

A softwood staircase is the preferred choice; a disadvantage of these staircases is the phenol-content of the bonding in laminated sustainable wood strings. Direct reuse is no problem with wooden and steel stairs. A sectional construction is preferred in all cases with regard to recycling. Steel as a material is problematic in view of the extraction of the raw materials, coal and iron ore, and the pollution caused in manufacture. Steel has a high energy content.

Concrete stairs are an obvious alternative for internal stairs in multi-storey buildings, when the supporting structure is also of a stone, concrete or brick material and the fire regulations prohibit the use of wood. We would recommend the use of concrete with reclaimed aggregate in this case. The scarcity of the raw materials used is also the reason to rank concrete in third place.

See Part 4 for a more detailed description of the environmental impact of the materials mentioned.

58

not recommended

The use of tropical, non-sustainable wood is not recommended on account of the depletion of the ecosystem.

basic selection

An internal staircase of European softwood is commonly used and cheap and has therefore been included in the basic selection.

comments

A softwood staircase is by far the cheapest of the alternatives mentioned. Different demands (such as for fire safety) are made of a staircase common to several dwellings than of an internal staircase within one dwelling. Often a common staircase is already installed during shell construction, which means the chosen building method has to be adapted.

External stairs

preference 1 sustainable durable wood	*preference 2* steel	*preference 3* concrete with reclaimed aggregate	*not recommended* tropical wood, preserved wood

environmental preference

An external staircase of durable wood is preferred because the material is renewable. Recycling offers no problems for steel and wooden stairs. Sectional attachment is preferred. In practice the choice of steel or concrete is based on functional and aesthetic demands. Steel is used for fire escapes in particular. These two variants are similar from an environmental point of view, as long as concrete with reclaimed aggregate is used. See Part 4 for a more detailed description of the environmental impact of the materials mentioned.

not recommended

The use of non-sustainable wood is not recommended on account of the impact on ecosystems. Wood preservatives should be avoided as much as possible, due to the leaching of harmful substances.

basic selection

Concrete (with reclaimed aggregate), as wooden external stairs are not always suitable.

comments

Fire regulations can prevent the use of wooden external stairs.

Internal balustrades/railings

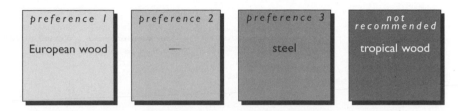

environmental preference

European softwood is preferable to steel for internal balustrades and rails. Steel is problematic due to the extraction of the raw materials, coal and iron ore, and also because of the pollution occurring in manufacture. See Part 4 for a more detailed description of the environmental impact of the materials mentioned.

not recommended

The use of non-sustainable for balustrades and rails is not recommended on account of damage to the ecosystem and the depletion of tropical rainforests.

basic selection

European wood is acceptable and cheap.

comments

Beech is a good possibility for railings because it is flexible and hard. The price of a beech railing is comparable to that of a hardwood railing. Softwood balustrades are a little cheaper than balustrades made of meranti or merbau. Steel stair-gates are dearest.

External balustrades/railings

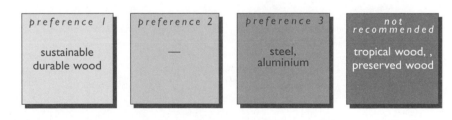

environmental preference

Durable wood is preferable to steel for external balustrades and rails. Steel, which is used externally, needs to be treated to prevent corrosion. Sectional steel elements can be reused primarily at a later stage.
The extraction and manufacture of aluminium causes heavy pollution, particularly because of its high energy content. Aluminium, like steel, is eminently recyclable.
See Part 4 for a more detailed description of the environmental impact of the materials mentioned.

not recommended

The use of non-sustainable wood in balustrades and rails is not recommended on account of the depletion of the ecosystems. Wood preservatives should be avoided if possible.

basic selection

Steel or aluminium. Balustrades made of durable wood are an obvious choice in combination with wooden stairs, although less so when in combination with a concrete staircase, which is the basic selection.

comments

Steel rails for an external staircase are somewhat cheaper than wooden rails.

For roof construction see 21–25

Environmental selection of materials for use in Construction

Pitched roof coverings

preference 1	preference 2	preference 3	not recommended
timber shingles, reed	clay or concrete roof tiles	fibre-cement slates, corrugated panels, bituminous slates	zinc, copper

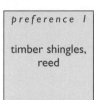

environmental preference

Timber shingles and reed are renewable, in contrast with the other options, and they are therefore the first choice for covering pitched roofs.

A preference for clay or concrete roof tiles cannot be expressed without further detailed research. The production of clay tiles requires a relatively large amount of energy. More harmful substances are emitted in their production, than during the manufacture of concrete tiles. The extraction of binding agents and the production of cement are the most environmentally damaging aspects of the manufacture of concrete tiles. The environmental effects of concrete and clay tiles balance each other out. Slates and corrugated sheets made of fibre cement contain more cement than do concrete tiles, and are less durable. Bituminous slates are a product of the petroleum processing industry.

See Part 4 for a more detailed description of the environmental impact of the materials mentioned.

not recommended

Sufficient alternatives are available for a pitched roof to eliminate the need for zinc and copper. The corrosion of these can lead to contamination of water and soil, with consequent damage to organisms. In addition zinc is a relatively scarce resource with a short life.

basic selection

Clay and concrete tiles are common and are therefore included in the basic selection.

comments

Reeds, as well as timber shingles, can cause problems in urban areas due to their flammability. Their use is at present recommended only in detached situations.
Concrete tiles are by far the cheapest, followed by ceramic tiles and slates. Timber shingles are considerably more expensive.

61

Flat roof coverings

preference 1	*preference 2*	*preference 3*	*not recommended*
—	EPDM sheet, modified bitumen felt (APP, SBS)	blown bitumen felt, recycled PVC, EPDM with bitumen layer	zinc, PVC

Fixing coverings

preference 1	*preference 2*	*preference 3*	*not recommended*
loose with plants	loose with gravel	mechanical	glued, bonded

environmental preference

Ethylene propylene diene monomer (EPDM) is an elastomeric, synthetic sheet material which can easily be reused, primarily when it is loose or has been mechanically attached. EPDM is longer-lasting than roofing felt made with blown bitumen.
Atactic polypropylene (APP) and styrene-butadiene-styrene (SBS) bitumen are the materials most commonly used in the manufacture of roofing felts. APP bitumen consists of about 70% bitumen and 30% of APP. SBS bitumen consists of 87% bitumen and 13% SBS. APP bitumen is in itself resistant to ultra-violet radiation, but SBS bitumen requires a mineralised coating. Both materials have a considerably longer life-span (about 20 years) than the 'usual' blown bitumen. Modified bitumen systems have few layers and are thinner than blown bitumen. One-coating bitumen is also often not fixed, which simplifies reuse.
The mixtures, consisting of a top layer of EPDM and a bitumen lower layer, cause problems during waste disposal if glued or bonded. 'Recycled PVC' means that a substantial fraction has been recycled. Alternatively, future recycling should be guaranteed.

By ballasting or mechanically attaching a roof covering, rather than bonding it, we can increase the opportunities for recycling. Ballasting protects the roof covering against the effects of the weather and in particular against ultra-violet radiation, which lengthens its life-span. Ballasting with sedum plants on a base of clay granules is preferable in view of the scarcity of gravel. Sedum plants are a kind of succulent, relatively impervious to arid conditions. A green roof has a water buffer capacity (helping to avoid the overloading of sewers) and improves the micro-climate in towns (dust attraction, humidity control). See Part 4 for a more detailed description of the environmental impact of the materials mentioned.

not recommended

The durability and recycling opportunities of sheet PVC are greater than those of bitumen. The pollution caused through sheet PVC production and the processing of PVC waste is, however, so great that bitumen still wins out. The production of zinc is relatively harmful and the metal is scarce. A substantial fraction of PVC should be recycled, or future recycling guaranteed.
Glueing or bonding roofing materials has the result that the material can no longer, (or only with difficulty) be separated from the insulation or roof structure, which causes problems for waste disposal. The production and application of solvent-based adhesives impedes health, as well as the environment.

basic selection

EPDM, APP and SBS bituminous roof covering are included in the basic selection.

comments

The additional costs of EPDM are quite high. A disadvantage of a green roof is that the structure must have a larger load-bearing capacity. This must be taken into account in the case of wooden roofs.

For sealants see 36

Glazing type

preference 1	preference 2	preference 3	not recommended
argon-filled LE-glazing	air-filled LE-glazing	double glazing	single glazing

environmental preference
By LE-glazing we mean low emissivity glazing, sometimes called Plus-glazing. LE-glazing (U =about 1.6) has a lower U-value than double glazing (U = 3) and single glazing (U = 5.7). LE-glazing with a coating of silver and an argon-filled cavity insulates best (U = 1.3). The energy savings outweigh any environmental threat from the use of cavity gas and the coating. LE-glazing should be used as much as possible to achieve significant energy savings.

not recommended
The use of single glazing in domestic dwellings is not recommended from the point of view of energy saving, as well as that of living comfort.

basic selection
LE-glazing for living rooms and double glazing for bedrooms.

comments
LE-glazing is at present still 25%– 35% dearer than double glazing. It is to be expected that the difference in price will decrease in view of the rapid increase in the use of LE-glazing. The introduction of an energy performance standard (EPN) could accelerate this. The additional costs of LE-glazing compared to double-glazing are repaid by the energy saving within its lifetime.

63

Installing glazing

preference 1	preference 2	preference 3	not recommended
dry glazing	semi-dry glazing	wet glazing	—

environmental preference
Dry glazing with a rubber sealant is preferable to other methods on account of its greater durability. Wet glazing with sealant or putty requires more maintenance. The maintenance cycle for semi-dry glazing, which combines a rubber seal inside the glass cavity with external wooden mouldings and sealant, lies between the other methods. Elastomeric sealants are preferable to plastic ones in view of their greater durability (see 36 *sealants*).

basic selection
Dry glazing is in the basic selection, but it is a little more expensive.

comments
Wooden mouldings are used when installing double and LE-glazing. They can have rubber seals and/or a sealant may be used. The material preference for the mouldings is similar to that of external frames and windows (see 30 *window frames*).

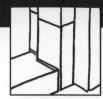

Thresholds

preference 1	preference 2	preference 3	not recommended
solid natural stone	ceramic tiles, manufactured stone	synthetic stone	—

environmental preference

Manufactured (cast) stone is more polluting than solid natural stone, due to the use of the bonding agents. Production of ceramic tiles requires more energy than the production of solid natural stone.
Synthetic stone is concrete which is not reinforced and to which double-figure percentages of polyester are added. The production process of polyester pollutes.

basic selection

Synthetic stone.

comments

A threshold made of tiles is much more expensive due to it being labour-intensive. A solid natural stone threshold is a little more expensive than a synthetic stone threshold.

Sealing joints

preference 1	*preference 2*	*preference 3*	*not recommended*
coconut fibre, felt, sisal	mineral wool, PE tape, EPDM seals	elastomeric sealant with base filler	PUR foam, PUR sealant

environmental preference

Renewable raw materials such as coconut fibre and felt can be used for sealing joints. They are products which have been processed only minimally and are therefore less environmentally damaging.

As a second choice we list products which are produced from non-renewable raw materials, but which have a limited impact on the environment with regard to their extraction and manufacture: polyethylene (PE) foam tape on a roll, mineral wool bands and ethylene propylene diene monomer (EPDM) synthetic rubber seals. The production process of PE results in a greater threat to the environment than that of mineral wool. The important point is that PE is not foamed with chlorofluorocarbons (CFCs). The solution, in which an elastomeric sealant is applied to a base filling, requires more maintenance that the other variants. Large amounts of sealant are involved, depending on the width of the join.

See Part 4 for a more detailed description of the environmental impact of the materials mentioned.

not recommended

The largest problem of polyurethane (PUR) foam is the propellant which is used for foaming. This uses CFCs which damage the ozone layer. At present other foaming agents, such as hydro-fluorocarbons, (H)CFCs, are often used, which are less of a threat to the ozone layer. The use of PUR sealant and PUR foam with an ozone-friendly foaming agent is not recommended, as a great many other deleterious substances are released in the production of PUR. PUR foam has the additional disadvantage that the strong adhesion impedes the reuse of the materials.

basic selection

The sealant to be applied depends on the functional demands being made. In most cases materials from preference 2 will be satisfactory. These materials would have been included in the basic selection were it not for the fact that the use of PUR cannot always be excluded in practice.

comments

The use of sealants for joints can be reduced by thoughtful specification and choice of building systems. The use of PUR foam in concrete element construction, for instance, is virtually impossible to avoid due to the required size tolerances.

The choice of a variant depends in practice on the functional demands being made, such as the degree of airtightness, whether shrinking and expanding can be accommodated, and whether it is affected by the weather. The application of coconut fibre or sisal for sealing a joint on the exterior wall is only possible if the material is covered by joinery. Sealing tape made of mineral wool is supplied on a roll. Joints wider than 15 mm can be covered by a double strip. Mineral wool can also be used for base fillings in combination with a finish of elastomeric sealants.

Sealing cracks

preference 1	preference 2	preference 3	not recommended
EPDM and EPT-rubber	—	PE tape	PVC and PUR tape

environmental preference

Rubber seals and foam tapes are suitable for sealing cracks. Polyethylene (PE) and PVC tape consist of respectively foamed PE and foamed PVC. The production process of PE is less polluting than that of PVC, and PE is also more degradable.
Ethylene propylene diene monomer (EPDM) and ethylene propylene terpolymer (EPT) rubber seals are comparable with PE tape with regard to pollution, but they have the advantage of a considerably longer life-span. See Part 4 for a more detailed description of the environmental impact of the materials mentioned.

not recommended

Tape foamed with (H)CFCs is not recommended because of the threat to the ozone layer. The use of CFC-free PVC tape is not recommended either, in view of the considerable threat to the environment PVC poses.

basic selection

PE tape is included in the basic selection. EPDM and EPT rubber is the basic choice for applications such as sealing pivoting windows.

comments

An additional problem of PVC foam tape is that PVC and acrylic paint bond and so cannot be used together.
PE tapes can be used for cracks of maximum 10 mm. The products suitable for sealing wider joints are described under 36 *sealing joints*.

66

Elastomeric sealants

preference 1	preference 2	preference 3	not recommended
silicone sealant	polysulphide sealant	—	PUR sealant

environmental preference

Silicone sealant contains silicones as bonding agents, as well as filler, pigment and added substances. The toxicity of silicone sealant is determined by the drying substances and the primers, which can irritate the skin in particular. Drying substances and primers are also a problem in polysulphide sealant. In addition, the occasional presence of lead can affect the brain and blood, as well as other parts of the human body. Not much is known about the toxicity of polysulphides (the bonding agent). Polysulphide sealant is very flammable, in contrast to silicone sealant.
See Part 4 for a more detailed description of the environmental impact of the materials mentioned.

not recommended

The toxicity of polyurethane (PUR) sealant is determined by the polyurethane components present, the primers (skin irritations) and tin alloys. Such sealants are not recommended in view of the toxicity of the PUR components.

basic selection

Polysulphide sealant is satisfactory and no dearer than PUR sealant; the disadvantage of silicone sealant is that it is not suitable for all situations.

comments

Where either plastic or elastomeric sealants can be used in a particular application, then elastomeric sealant has the advantage of being longer-lasting (8–15 years) than plastic sealant (2–10 years). This leads to a reduced requirement of sealant over a certain period. Natural (plastic) sealant however is so much less polluting that natural sealant is preferred to elastic sealant despite its shorter life-span.

The various sealants cannot be used as a matter of course in all cases. The use of silicone sealant for glazing, for instance, is not advised on account of the strong bonding.

Plastic sealants

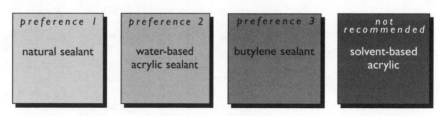

preference 1	preference 2	preference 3	not recommended
natural sealant	water-based acrylic sealant	butylene sealant	solvent-based acrylic

environmental preference

Natural sealants are made from renewable raw materials, with water as the solvent. The production process does not threaten the environment. The sealant degrades well as waste. Acrylic sealants, which do not contain organic solvents, but water instead, do not affect health.

Butylene sealant contains a bonding agent which is less harmful. Other components are fillers, pigments and hardening substances. The threat from these components is small. The toxicity is determined by the aliphatic and aromatic solvents, which are present in small quantities.

See Part 4 for a more detailed description of the environmental impact of the materials mentioned.

not recommended

The toxicity of acrylic sealant which is not water-based is determined mainly by the aromatic solvents, which may give headaches and narcotic effects amongst others. These solvents are also flammable. Remnants of acrylic monomer in the bonding agent can also have a sensitising effect. The use of these sealants is not recommended in view of the threats which the solvents pose.

basic selection

The use of water-based acrylic sealant is technically comparable to, and no more expensive than alternatives which are a greater threat.

comments

Natural sealant is more expensive than the other sealants.

Plasterwork

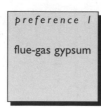

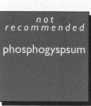

preference 1	*preference 2*	*preference 3*	*not recommended*
flue-gas gypsum	lime mortar	natural gypsum	phosphogyspsum

environmental preference

Gypsum gained from electricity power plants is preferable to natural gypsum and lime mortar for internal plasterwork because this gypsum is a by-product. Extraction poses no additional threat to the environment and recycling prevents the dumping of waste. Lime requires little processing, which results in a relatively pollution-free production process. Less energy is required than in the manufacture of natural gypsum mortar.
See Part 4 for a more detailed description of the environmental impact of the materials mentioned.

not recommended

Phosphogypsum, a by-product from the artificial fertiliser industry, can emit radiation. The risk of radiation from plasterwork is less than from sheets or blocks due to its limited thickness, nevertheless phosphogypsum is not recommended for plasterwork.

basic selection

Natural gypsum is included in the basic selection; it is generally available. Gypsum from power plants may also become generally available soon (availability may differ throughout Europe) due in part to opposition to the extraction of natural gypsum in Germany.

External wall rendering

preference 1	*preference 2*	*preference 3*	*not recommended*
ceramic tiles	mineral render	synthetic render	—

environmental preference

Ceramic tiles have the advantage of a considerably longer life-span than a layer of render. They can also be separated from the insulation layer in the waste phase. Mineral render also contains synthetics, but less than synthetic render, which contains about 10% synthetics. The mixing of synthetics with stone, concrete or brick contaminates construction and demolition waste.

basic selection

Mineral rendering is technically comparable to synthetic rendering, or better, and the additional expense is negligible.

comments

Rendered external walls are generally painted. The removal of dirt and the maintenance of the paintwork means that the environment is more or less polluted, depending on the materials chosen. Mineral rendering attracts less dirt than synthetic rendering.

Fitting tiles

preference 1

bedding in
mineral mortar

preference 2

natural adhesive

preference 3

water-based
adhesive

*not
recommended*

solvent-based
adhesive

environmental preference

Tiles can be fitted to a concrete base when a mineral mortar screed or render is applied (monolithic bedding). Manufacture of the screed or render does not cause much pollution and the consumption of scarce raw materials is limited, because sand forms a large proportion of the mortar.
Natural adhesives are made from natural and degradable materials. The production process of the adhesives is relatively clean.
Water-based adhesives cause pollution in their production process, however, and the waste from the adhesives is also a pollutant. A significant advantage over solvent-based adhesives is that they contain either few or no organic solvents at all.
See Part 4 for a more detailed description of the environmental impact of the materials mentioned.

not recommended

The toxicity of solvent-based adhesives used for fixing tiles depends on the organic solvents in particular. These solvents are flammable, and many harmful substances are released during their manufacture. The use of such adhesives, especially for large surfaces, is therefore not recommended.

basic selection

Bedding in mineral mortar is included in the basic selection for fixing floor tiles, and water-based adhesive for wall tiles.

comments

The remnants and packaging of adhesives must be regarded as chemical waste.
Tiling walls by bedding in mortar is considerably more labour-intensive than fixing with adhesive, which makes it about 30% more expensive. This cost difference can increase when tilers are scarce.

69

Floor screeds

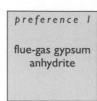

preference 1	preference 2	preference 3	not recommended
flue-gas gypsum anhydrite	natural gypsum anhydrite	sand cement	phosphogypsum anhydrite

environmental preference

Anhydrite is a plaster mortar which is suitable for floor screeds. The environmental effects of the extraction and production of natural gypsum and the raw materials for a sand-cement mortar are comparable. The preference for anhydrite to sand cement is due to its ease of application. Anhydrite is very fluid and can be applied simply with a hose, after which it is self-levelling. The smoothing down of a sand-cement floor screed is physically hard work.

Radiation from the flue-gas gypsum is even lower than that from natural gypsum. Dumping of waste is avoided with the use of flue-gas gypsum. There is no question of extraction, in contrast to the variants, so the landscape is not affected. Anhydrite made from flue-gas gypsum therefore is preferred to natural anhydrite and sand-cement.

See Part 4 for a more detailed description of the environmental impact of the materials mentioned.

not recommended

An anhydrite floor made of phosphogypsum is not recommended due to its level of radiation.

Phosphogypsum, as well as gypsum gained from electricity power plants, is an industrial waste product. Phosphogypsum however can emit relatively intense radioactive radiation, whereas the radiation from the flue-gas gypsum is even lower than that of natural gypsum. Some phosphogypsum also has a high degree of heavy metals, including cadmium.

basic selection

Anhydrite made from flue-gas gypsum is included in the basic selection. It is technically uncontroversial, there are significant environmental benefits, and only limited additional costs.

comments

Anhydrite screeds can be used for suspended floor screeds and as a screed for wooden floors. There is hardly any shrinkage, there is not much risk of cracking, and the material is self-sealing.

A disadvantage of anhydrite, compared with concrete, is that the screed must be separated from the concrete floor during demolition. Concrete contaminated with plaster is not suitable for reuse as reclaimed aggregate. An anhydrite floor can be laid on top of polyethylene (PE) membrane in order to facilitate separation in the waste phase. The additional environmental burden of PE membrane is smaller than the environmental gain at this later stage.

Anhydrite floors are still somewhat more expensive than sand-cement floors. The more favourable working conditions, in particular, reduce the price difference. The fact that pouring anhydrite is faster than smoothing out a sand-cement screed contributes to this.

Bathroom and toilet floors

preference I

granitic
(terrazzo)

preference 2

ceramic tiles

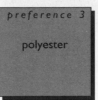
preference 3

polyester

not
recommended

PVC

environmental preference

A granitic floor, also called terrazzo, is a poured concrete floor to which natural stone has been added, giving the appearance of granite. The composition and finish of the floor is such that it is smooth, hard and waterproof. An advantage of a granitic floor is that no sealant is needed to make the wall junctions waterproof as the floor can have a raised lip at its edges. (This in contrast to a tiled floor.) If, however, sealant is used then the placing of the sealant is much less critical than for a tiled floor. No adhesive is required for fitting tiles. The durability of the granitic floor is greater than that of the other materials and the risk of leakage is smaller. A tiled floor is preferred to a polyester floor. Polyester causes considerable pollution throughout its life cycle, from extraction to waste disposal. The life-span of a polyester shower floor is also limited.
See Part 4 for a more detailed description of the environmental impact of the materials mentioned.

not recommended

The use of PVC floor finish is not recommended. A PVC floor finish is vulnerable to mechanical influences, as well as being a pollutant.

basic selection

Ceramic tile finish for the floor as well as the walls is common and therefore included in the basic selection.

comments

A granitic floor is more expensive than the alternatives, but the elimination of sealant and tile finish results in it being maintenance-free.

Environmental selection of materials for use in Construction

Wall and ceiling framing systems

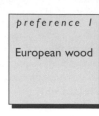

preference 1	preference 2	preference 3	not recommended
European wood	steel	aluminium	—

environmental preference

Wood is a renewable material and does not cause problems for waste disposal because it degrades well.

The extraction and production of aluminium pollutes more than that of steel. Aluminium and steel can be reused, therefore the difference between them and native softwood becomes less significant.

See Part 4 for a more detailed description of the environmental impact of the materials mentioned.

basic selection

Wood is included in the basic selection as a material for wall and ceiling framing systems.

comments

A panelled frame for a ceiling system has the advantage that a sound-insulating layer can be applied between the panels and the ceiling. Another advantage is improved acoustics.

72

Wall and ceiling panelling systems

preference 1	preference 2	preference 3	not recommended
flue-gas gypsum board	natural gypsum, fibreboard made of wood wool magnesite, wood wool cement or flax	sustainable plywood, mineral wool board, chipboard	phosphogypsum board

environmental preference

Flue-gas gypsum is a by-product from coal-fired electricity plants. The extraction of natural gypsum and magnesite causes environmental damage. The production of gypsum plasterboard and gypsum fibreboard uses no environmentally harmful adhesives, in contrast to the production of flax fibreboard and plywood. Bonded types of board, woodwool magnesite, woodwool cement and sustainable plywood are largely made of renewable raw materials. The regeneration of flax is greater, therefore flax fibreboard is preferred to plywood. The extraction of bonding agents for the woodwool board (magnesite and binding agents) damages the landscape.

A mineral wool board also has a sound-insulating effect. The degradability of mineral wool is poor and its fibres can irritate skin and mucous membranes when this material is being worked with.

See Part 4 for a more detailed description of the environmental impact of the materials mentioned.

not recommended

Phosphogypsum is a by-product of the artificial fertiliser industry. The proportion of harmful substances is generally so high that the use of phosphogypsum indoors presents a risk and is not recommended.

basic selection	Natural gypsum board is included in the basic selection for the wall as well as for ceiling finishes. It is easily available and can be used at low cost.
comments	Mineral wool board, woodwool cement board and woodwool magnesite board are unsuitable for wall panels. There is a difference between gypsum plasterboard on the one hand and gypsum fibreboard on the other: gypsum plasterboard consists of a core of gypsum, which is covered with a cardboard skin on each side to strengthen it. Gypsum fibreboard, however, stands up better to mechanical forces than plasterboard. This is considered important, and so it would be preferable to use gypsum fibreboard. At the time of writing, flue-gas gypsum board is about 10% more expensive than natural gypsum board. The price of natural gypsum, however, is rising due to stricter conditions being imposed on its extraction in Germany. If acoustic demands are set, then woodwool magnesite or woodwool cement panels are a good choice for ceiling panels.

73

For preservative treatments see 06
For paintwork see 46
For panelling see 44

Environmental selection of materials for use in Construction

Internal joinery

preference 1	*preference 2*	*preference 3*	*not recommended*
European wood	chipboard, sustainable plywood	fibre cement	PVC, tropical wood

environmental preference

Durability is not important for internal woodwork as the risk of damage by fungi or insects is minimal. Untreated softwood is satisfactory and is a renewable material which is degradable. European softwood has the advantage that its transport occurs over short distances, which keeps the energy content low.

With plywood however, harmful adhesives are used for bonding the different veneer layers together to form the material. This accounts for the material's lower ranking. The adhesive used in chipboard is also problem because even high-specification chipboard can incorporate an adhesive which contains formaldehyde. The risk to human health is such that the use of chipboard should be avoided for larger surfaces. The share of bonding agents (cement) in fibre cement is 25% The energy content and damage to the landscape during extraction are its most important environmental aspects. There is no need to use durable wood.

See Part 4 for a more detailed description of the environmental impact of the materials mentioned.

not recommended

The use of non-sustainable wood and PVC is not recommended.

basic selection

European softwood is satisfactory and cheap, and is therefore included in the basic selection.

comments

European softwood is cheap to buy. It is commonly painted however, which is labour-intensive and damaging to the environment. This and the additional material used for painting makes it a more expensive alternative. PVC skirting boards are used particularly as a cable duct for electrical and computer cables.

74

External joinery

preference 1	*preference 2*	*preference 3*	*not recommended*
sustainable durable wood	painted European wood	sustainable plywood	tropical wood, preserved wood

environmental preference

Durable woods are preferred in damp situations as they require no wood preservatives. The vulnerability of this material can be limited by proper fixing and protecting the timber ends. Less durable woods can also be used in that case. Native softwood is preferable to durable woods for applications where damp has little significance. Durable wood generally needs to be transported over longer distances, as well. The layers of veneer in plywood are bonded with harmful adhesives which determine the degree of environmental pollution it causes.
Harmful wood preservatives are not needed if the right materials are chosen and the specification is well thought out.
See Part 4 for a more detailed description of the environmental impact of the materials mentioned.

not recommended

The use of non-sustainable wood is not recommended.

basic selection

Painted softwood is included in the basic selection: it is suitable in nearly every instance, and is relatively cheap (see 46 *paintwork*).

comments

See Part 4 for examples of durable woods.

Interior paintwork (wood)

preference 1	preference 2	preference 3	not recommended
untreated wax, water-based natural stain	water-based acrylic paint	natural paint, high-solids alkyd paint	alkyd paint

Exterior paintwork (wood)

preference 1	preference 2	preference 3	not recommended
natural paint, boiled paint	high-solids alkyd paint	water-based acrylic paint	alkyd paint

environmental preference

There is no need to preserve wood which is only used internally. A natural wax, such as beeswax, can be used if internal woodwork must be treated. Such a wax is made of renewable raw ingredients. A water-based natural stain has recently come on the market which is produced from renewable materials and which has a low percentage of solvents. Water-based acrylic paints contain less organic solvent than alkyd paints, (2%–7%, compared with 40%–50%). Water-based acrylic paints have the disadvantage that more harmful additives, such as biocides and emulsifiers, are added. The composition of the high-solids paints is comparable to that of common alkyd-resin paints. The percentage of harmful organic solvents is considerably lower, being at about only 20%.

Natural paint is mostly manufactured from renewable materials, but it does contain about 30%–55% solvents, e.g. turpentine, which are damaging to human health, particularly that of the painter when working indoors.

See Part 4 for a more detailed description of the environmental impact of the materials mentioned.

not recommended

The greatest disadvantage of the commonly used alkyd paints are the organic solvents (40%–50%) which threaten the health of the painter and reduce the quality of the air.

basic selection

Natural paint and high-solids alkyd paint for interior woodwork and high-solids alkyd paint for outside.

comments

Remnants of all paints must be treated as chemical waste. Natural paints are more expensive than the alternatives. Unfamiliarity with the application and the slower drying make it more costly to use in practice. The authors are aware that manufacturers of natural paint are trying to reduce the percentage of solvents.

The drying time of high-solids paint is also longer than that of the commonly used alkyd paint This can cause problems in mass production due to a lack of drying space.

Boiled paint is a favourable alternative for wooden external wall cladding (see Part 4).

Wood/stone joints

preference 1	*preference 2*	*preference 3*	*not recommended*
natural preservative	water-based or high-solids primer	iron red lead, alkyd resin primer	lead red lead

environmental preference

A natural preservative is preferable for the treatment of wood which is in contact with concrete, stone or brick. Natural preservatives make the wood water-repellent and protect it from attack. The preservative is relatively harmless and degradable. Primers contain harmful substances, similar to other synthetic paints, but the percentage of filler is greater and therefore the proportion of solvents is proportionally lower. The filler is not normally very harmful.

Red leads are also regarded as primers, to which lead or iron oxide have been added. The effect of the iron oxide in iron red lead is mainly visual.

A similar quality of protection can be achieved with primer based on alkyd resin. Water-based and high-solids primers contain smaller amounts of organic solvents than iron and lead red lead, but iron red lead is preferable to lead red lead because lead is harmful.

See Part 4 for a more detailed description of the environmental impact of the materials mentioned.

not recommended

Lead red lead contains a considerable quantity of lead, which is harmful to health. The use of lead is not recommended.

basic selection

A high-solids or water-based primer is included in the basic selection. The protective effect is similar to that of the more common iron red lead, and the additional costs are negligible.

Surface preparation
(walls)

preference 1	*preference 2*	*preference 3*	*not recommended*
none	natural preservative	water-based preservative	solvent-based preservative

Interior paintwork
(walls)

preference 1	*preference 2*	*preference 3*	*not recommended*
whitewash	mineral paint, water-based natural stain	natural paint, water-based acrylic paint	alkyd paint

Exterior paintwork
(walls)

preference 1	*preference 2*	*preference 3*	*not recommended*
mineral paint, water-based natural stain	natural paint	water-based acrylic paint	alkyd paint

environmental preference

An undercoat is not always necessary to prevent paint from being absorbed by the wall. If one is applied, then a natural preservative is preferable because they are not very harmful and are degradable. A water-based primer contains less organic solvent, but does have a number of polluting and badly degradable components.

Whitewash is our first choice for internal wall paint. The production of whitewash comprises lime dissolved in water with no further additions. Limestone or shells must be extracted and burnt for the production of whitewash, which is a relatively clean process. Mineral and water-based paints use water as a solvent. An advantage of mineral paint is that it contains few synthetics, and it covers surfaces in a single layer so that less paint is needed.

A disadvantage with natural paints, compared with mineral paints, is that organic solvents are released which can be a threat to health when used indoors.

See Part 4 for a more detailed description of the environmental impact of the materials mentioned.

not recommended

The use of materials containing solvents is not recommended. The composition of alkyd-based wall paints is similar to that of alkyd paints for wood.

basic selection

For the preparation of walls, if necessary, use a water-based paint.
For internal walls use water-based paint.
For external walls use mineral paint.

comments

Whitewash is less impervious to water than to other wall paints, which can be an advantage. A disadvantage with whitewash is that it is not very smudge-proof. Remnants of water-based wall paints must also be treated as chemical waste. Rinsing brushes and other tools under the tap, for instance, causes a lot of pollution.

Ferrous metal paintwork

preference I	preference 2	preference 3	not recommended
natural paint, duplex system	high-solids alkyd paint	alkyd paint, iron red lead	lead red lead, epoxy-alkyd systems, thermal galvanising

environmental preference

Duplex galvanising is achieved by applying a powder coating as a finishing to a thermally galvanised surface. The powder coating is applied electrolytically in the factory, which means that no solvents are used and little paint is spilled. The life-span of a duplex galvanised coating is considered to be rather longer than that of a thermal layer of zinc. The powder coating prevents leaching of zinc to the soil, and the advantage, compared with other paint systems, is that no layers of paint need to be applied during its life-time, as well as a reduction in solvents.
Steel could in principle be treated with alkyd or natural paint. Natural paint is made of natural raw materials, but it contains a high proportion of natural solvents. A high-solids alkyd paints is preferable to common alkyd paint due to its lower solvent content.
See Part 4 for a more detailed description of the environmental impact of the materials mentioned.

not recommended

Thermal galvanising must be avoided for outdoor use as zinc leaches when water flows over it. The leaching is more severe in aggressive environments, and zinc is also vulnerable to damage, for example when tightening fasteners. A damaged zinc layer can be painted over, however, but treatment with an environmentally damaging primer is necessary.
The use of lead red lead is also not advised, because lead is so harmful to human health. Paint systems based on epoxy are not recommended due to harmful emissions occurring during the production process and the effects on the health of the worker.

basic selection

Duplex galvanising is a common practice, but it is expensive compared with the alternatives. We have therefore included a high-solids alkyd paint as a basic alternative.

Kitchen units/cupboards

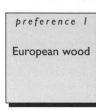

preference 1	preference 2	preference 3	not recommended
European wood	sustainable plywood	chipboard, fibreboard	plywood made from tropical wood

environmental preference

Solid, non-tropical wood has the advantage that it does not contain adhesives.
Plywood contains less adhesive and is longer-lasting than chipboard.
The bonding in chipboard poses more problems than that of the other alternatives. The production of adhesives itself releases many harmful substances. Chipboard is also faced with a synthetic layer (melamine) which impedes efficient waste disposal.
See Part 4 for a more detailed description of the environmental impact of the materials mentioned.

not recommended

The use of tropical plywood is not recommended.

basic selection

There is no basic selection as alternatives to chipboard are at present still too expensive for regular use in the construction of domestic buildings.

comments

The difference in price between kitchen units made of chipboard and those made of solid wood is typically a factor of four. This means that in practice, particularly in social housing construction, it is not financially feasible to avoid using chipboard. There is, however, some hope that affordable kitchen units will be developed which do not make use of chipboard.

Work surfaces

preference 1	preference 2	preference 3	not recommended
beech	granitic finish, stainless steel	synthetic resin board, synthetic stone	chipboard faced with melamine

environmental preference

Wood normally has the advantage that it is a renewable raw material, that little pollution is caused in processing and that it does not cause problems for waste disposal. A granitic working surface, also called terrazzo, is a concrete slab which incorporates a natural stone. The composition and finish is smooth, hard and waterproof. The production process of a granitic working surface is cleaner and costs less energy than that of synthetic stone and synthetic resin board. Synthetic resin bonded boards cause problems for waste disposal, unlike the other products. A stainless steel work surface can be reused at the end of its useful life. The stainless steel top is easily separated from the plywood base.
See Part 4 for a more detailed description of the environmental impact of the materials mentioned.

not recommended

Chipboard faced with melamine is a pollutant on account of the large amount of bonding material it contains.

basic selection   A stainless steel work surface is somewhat cheaper than a synthetic resin bonded work surface. and is therefore included in the basic set.

comments   Steel and synthetic resin bonded work surfaces are much cheaper than those of beech or granitic finish. Work surfaces bonded with synthetic resin seem in practice to have an advantage over the variants in that the occupants can choose the colour.

Environmental selection of materials for use in *Construction*

Wallcoverings

preference 1	preference 2	preference 3	not recommended
paper	—	—	vinyl-coated paper

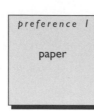

environmental preference Paper is based on cellulose, which is a renewable, degradable product. The production process of wallpaper is relatively clean.

not recommended The use of vinyl wallcovering coated with PVC is not recommended.

basic selection Wallpaper is widely used and cheap.

comments An advantage of wallpaper is that it is easy to paint over. An advantage of vinyl wallcovering is that it can be cleaned with water.

Floor coverings

preference 1	preference 2	preference 3	not recommended
linoleum	ceramic tiles	—	vinyl

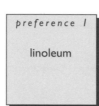

environmental preference Linoleum is preferable to tiles as a floor covering in rooms. Linoleum consists of renewable raw materials, such as cork, linseed oil and jute, and its degradability is good, depending on the finish.
Ceramic tiles are made of the less renewable material clay, with additives for, among other purposes, colour and hardness. They have a much greater energy content because of the firing process, and offer the advantage of being harder and therefore less vulnerable to damage.

not recommended The use of vinyl containing PVC is not recommended.

basic selection Ceramic tiles are included in the basic selection because linoleum is, in certain situations, insufficiently durable.

comments An advantage of floor coverings compared with a hard floor of wood or stone-like material is the sound insulation it offers. This reduces noise pollution to neighbouring houses or dwellings located below. Linoleum is more expensive than vinyl, but it lasts longer.

For lining a timber gutter see 31

Gutters

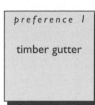

preference 1	preference 2	preference 3	not recommended
timber gutter	polyester	coated aluminium, recycled PVC	PVC, zinc, copper

environmental preference

Timber gutters and those made of polyester, coated aluminium and PVC do not corrode. The production processes for aluminium and PVC guttering are more environmentally damaging, than those for timber and lined gutters. This is true to a lesser extent for polyester guttering. Coated aluminium guttering is long-lasting and has a high-grade reuse value. 'Recycled PVC' means that a substantial fraction has been recycled. Alternatively, future recycling should be guaranteed

not recommended

The problem with zinc and copper guttering is corrosion, leading to contamination of the waste water or soil with zinc or copper. This is harmful to water quality and organisms in particular. In addition zinc is a scarce resource and has a relatively short life. PVC roof gutters give rise to considerable pollution during the production stage and as a waste.

basic selection

A lined timber gutter is much more expensive than a polyester one. The latter is therefore recommended for the basic selection.

comments

It is possible to eliminate the use of a gutter, which is primarily the first choice. This could be done by the use of a green roof, for example, preferably combined with a large overhang. The fixing of shingle pit strips under the roof overhang is desirable. The roof overhang also has a favourable effect in that it protects the external wall woodwork. A wooden gutter construction is about twice as expensive as a polyester gutter. The copper gutter is about 20% more expensive than the polyester gutter.

83

Gutter linings

preference 1	preference 2	preference 3	not recommended
EPDM, modified bitumen	blown bitumen	polyester	PVC, zinc, lead

environmental preference

The advantage of a gutter lined with ethylene propylene diene monomer (EPDM) is that it is durable. The production process of EPDM is less polluting than that of blown bitumen. The production of bituminous products, however, causes considerable pollution, from the extraction of petroleum, via the refining process up to and including waste disposal. However, modified bitumen has a greater life-span and less material is required.
See Part 4 for a more detailed description of the environmental impact of the materials mentioned.

not recommended

The use of PVC, zinc and lead is not recommended. Lead is an extremely toxic material for humans and the environment. The problem with zinc is corrosion leading to contamination of the waste water or soil with zinc This is harmful to water and organisms in particular. In addition zinc is a scarce resource with a relatively short life.

basic selection

A gutter lined with EPDM is included in the basic selection in view of the minimal absolute additional cost.

Drainpipes

preference 1

PE,
PP

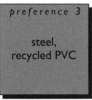

preference 2

polyester

preference 3

steel,
recycled PVC

not recommended

PVC,
copper

environmental preference

Synthetic pipes do not corrode and their production processes are less environmentally damaging than those of steel, copper and PVC. 'Recycled PVC' means that a substantial fraction has been recycled. Alternatively future recycling should be guaranteed
The production processes of polyethylene (PE) and polypropylene (PP) pollute least.

not recommended

The problem with copper pipes is corrosion, leading to contamination of waste water with copper. This is harmful to water organisms in particular. PVC down-pipes give rise to considerable pollution during the production stage and as waste.

basic selection

PP can be used in all cases with negligible additional costs compared with PVC, and is therefore included in the basic selection.

comments

PE drainpipes warp when exposed to direct sunlight and can therefore only be used in shielded locations. PP drainpipes are now available in a form which is resistant to ultra-violet radiation, making brittle pipes a thing of the past. A PP drainpipe is about 10% more expensive than a PVC one. Copper is much more expensive, but lasts longer and has recycling value.

84

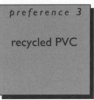

Internal waste systems

preference 1

ceramic

preference 2

PP,
PE

preference 3

recycled PVC

not recommended

PVC

environmental preference

The production process of ceramic pipes is considerably cleaner than that of synthetic pipes. The pipes cause few problems for disposal as waste.
Polypropylene (PP) and polyethylene (PE) score again more favourably than polyvinyl chloride (PVC) with regard to these aspects. In addition PP and PE are not bonded in contrast to PVC, but are attached with clamp connections. This not only eliminates the use of harmful adhesives, but also increases opportunities for reuse. 'Recycled PVC' means that a substantial fraction has been recycled. Alternatively, future recycling should be guaranteed.
See Part 4 for a more detailed description of the environmental impact of the materials mentioned.

not recommended

Problems with the production, as well as the waste disposal of PVC are greater than they are with PP. The use of non-recycled PVC is not recommended.

basic selection

PE and PP prove to be low cost compared with PVC and have therefore been included in the basic selection.

85

comments

The present generation of ceramic pipes can be used for more applications than previously because of the flexible connections used and diameters. Ceramic sewage pipes are unfortunately not available in small diameters. Prices for the alternatives differ little, although the fixings for ceramic pipes are more expensive. This is only partly the case for PP pipes which, to prevent sagging, require a few more brackets than for more rigid pipes.

Water supply

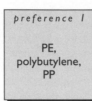

preference 1

PE,
polybutylene,
PP

preference 2

stainless steel

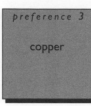

preference 3

copper

not recommended

—

environmental preference

The problem with copper pipes is corrosion, leading to contamination of the waste water with copper. This is harmful to water organisms in particular. This problem is not offset by the fact that copper has a high grade of reusability. Corrosion also occurs to a lesser extent in stainless steel. Synthetic pipes do not corrode and their production processes are less polluting than those for copper and stainless steel.

basic selection

There are sufficient alternatives to copper water pipes.

comments

The use of polyethylene (PE) and polybutylene for water pipes is still uncommon. Polybutylene and polypropylene (PP) are suitable for hot, as well as cold water pipes. PE can only be used for cold water pipes.

86

WC suites

preference 1	*preference 2*	*preference 3*	*not recommended*
Gustavsberg WSS system	adjustable flush	choice of flush	fixed flush

environmental preference

The Gustavsberg WSS system is a WC suite with a flow enlarger, and where the waste water drainage is such that only 4 litres of water are needed per flush (see Appendix 2 for suppliers). A siphon in the horizontal pipes – which lets the total water quantity through after about 20 flushes – is needed for each 10–12 dwellings. The use of this system is especially attractive in multi-storey constructions.
A cistern in which the flush depends on the length of time the flush button is depressed, enables the user to determine the exact amount of flushing water used. Another possibility is the use of a cistern which allows a choice between 3 and 6 litres of water.

not recommended

A fixed quantity of flushing water of 6 or 9 litres leads to a waste of water. The use of PVC for the WC cistern is not recommended.

basic selection

An adjustable flushing system or choice-based flushing system with a maximum flush volume of 6 litres is included in the basic selection. The additional costs are negligible.

comments

The WC bowls must have an adapted shape to be able to limit the flushing water quantities. The cost of a water-saving WC is approximately the same as a traditional WC. The additional costs of the Gustavsberg system are approximately the equivalent of £65–£85 per dwelling, depending on the number of dwellings connected per siphon. (The Gustavsberg system is not available in the UK at the time of writing.)

87

Taps and shower heads

preference 1	*preference 2*	*preference 3*	*not recommended*
water-saving	—	standard	—

environmental preference

Water-saving shower heads and taps with flow limiters enable a reduction in the use of tap water and energy consumption without a loss of comfort. The measure of flow can be regulated so as to achieve the desirable amount for the respective tap. This is usually somewhat more for kitchen taps than for a washbasin tap, respectively 6–8 litres per minute and 5–7 litres per minute. Some water-saving shower heads have an adapted internal design which, when combined with a built-in flow limiter, saves water without any loss of comfort.

basic selection

A water-saving shower head and water-saving tap are included in the basic selection.

comments

Flow limiters which are not vulnerable to scale are preferred in regions with hard water. We would advise using flow limiters which work independently of the pressure. However, the use of flow limiters is not possible for all types of domestic hot water installation. The tap threshold of the equipment must not fall below a certain value, because otherwise the equipment will not start.

A widespread misunderstanding is the use of perlators as a water-saving measure. Perlators introduce air into the water, giving the impression that a fuller flow is coming from the tap. In fact no saving of water occurs unless perlators are used in combination with flow limiters.

The additional costs incurred when installing water-saving taps and shower heads can be recovered within six months, where water is metered.

Heating installation

preference 1	*preference 2*	*preference 3*	*not recommended*
solar boiler + condensing boiler	condensing boiler	high-efficiency boiler	standard boiler

Provision of domestic hot water

preference 1	*preference 2*	*preference 3*	*not recommended*
solar boiler + condensing boiler	condensing combination boiler	high-efficiency combination boiler	standard combi boiler, any electric water heating

89

environmental preference

A solar water-heating system achieves the greatest saving of energy. A condition, however, is that supplementary heating is gas-fired. Solar boiler installations currently on the market are suitable only for heating domestic hot water, not for space heating. The latter demands a large collector surface and a large storage tank. The problem with this is that most of the heat gain is achieved during seasons when the need for space heating is minimal.

The savings which a condensing boiler provides are much greater than those of a high-efficiency boiler. In both cases, a low-NO_x boiler is preferred on account of its less harmful emissions. It is often advantageous, from an energy-saving point of view, to choose a heating installation which also supplies the domestic hot water.

not recommended

The use of conventional boilers is not recommended. The use of high-efficiency appliances or condensing boilers is necessary in order to achieve a high level of energy saving.

The energy content of electrically-heated water is much higher than that of water heated by gas. The use of any form of electrical water heating is therefore not recommended.

basic selection

Gas-fired condensing combination boilers are included in the basic selection for space heating and the provision of domestic hot water. The cost of this boiler is still considerably higher than that of the high-efficiency boiler, but it is balanced out by savings which make up the additional cost within several years.

comments

The choice of installation depends on the circumstances.

A preference for central heating rather than localised heating cannot be given. It may be attractive to heat smaller dwellings with individual heaters. Consideration should also be given as to whether the heating power which can be gained from industrial waste present in local districts could be used, or other energy-from-waste measures.

In the Netherlands, the additional costs of a solar boiler installation in a new building currently amount to about Dfl 3000 (£1100) per installation, including subsidies. Sometimes the distance between the location of the installation and the tap point is extremely large. A long pipe results in the loss of energy and water.

Insulation of pipes

preference 1	preference 2	preference 3	not recommended
cork	mineral wool	polyether	extruded polystyrene, PUR

environmental preference

Cork insulation offers the advantage that the raw material is renewable, its extraction uses little energy, and it is relatively clean. The waste is also degradable.
More energy is needed for the production of mineral wool, and it degrades into harmful products. Skin and mucous membranes have to be protected if mineral wool is being applied because fibres released during this process lead to irritation. Pollution as a result of the use of polyether is less than that of PUR. A mechanical attachment of the insulation shells with wire or clips is preferable to glueing.
See Part 4 for a more detailed description of the environmental impact of the materials mentioned.

not recommended

PUR causes pollution which is greater than that of mineral wool and polyether. The use of (H)CFCs as foaming agents for extruded polystyrene and PUR is therefore not recommended in view of the damage they cause to the ozone layer.

basic selection

Mineral wool is included in the basic selection because it is a commonly used material.

comments

A reduction in the loss of heat in hot water pipes does not always balance out the extra pollution caused by the use of insulation materials, compared with central heating pipes. This is, however, the case when the pipes cross unheated spaces. Cellulose is preferable as an insulation material for service ducts not only because of the secondary characteristic of the material, but also because of its sound insulation and fire-resistant properties. To this end a flame retardant is added.

Mains trunking

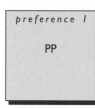

preference 1

PP

preference 2

—

preference 3

PVC

not recommended

—

environmental preference

The production of polypropylene (PP) is less polluting than that of PVC. An important advantage of PP is that chlorine is not used in the product. In decomposition PP causes also less pollution than polyvinyl chloride (PVC). See Part 4 for a more detailed description of the environmental impact of the materials mentioned.

not recommended

The use of PVC cannot be avoided in this application (see comments).

basic selection

As no alternative for PVC is available, this building element is not included in the basic selection.

comments

A manufacturer is engaged in the development of trunking made of PP.

91

Part 3

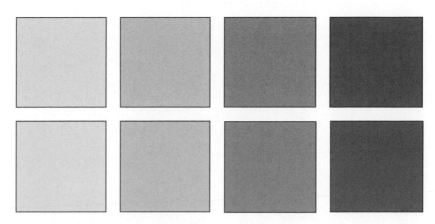

Environmental selection of materials for use in *Refurbishment*

Contents of Part 3: Environmental selection of materials for use in *Refurbishment*

**Building and
demolition waste**

preference 1	*preference 2*	*preference 3*	*not recommended*
separate all types	as preference 3 + wood, glass and synthetics	clean rubble, lowgrade chemical waste, metal and remainder	unseparated landfill

environmental preference

The separation of building and demolition waste created by refurbishment, opens up opportunities for further use. Reuse saves material and reduces dumping and incineration. Primary reuse, where the material is used again following either negligible or no further treatment, is preferable. Secondary reuse (recycling) where the released materials are reprocessed (smelting, breaking) in a reprocessing plant to form new materials requires additional transport and energy consumption and results in the release of harmful substances.
Incineration releases many noxious substances. A number of waste categories, such as wood and synthetic materials, generate energy when incinerated, in the form of heat. However, the environmental benefits from reuse are substantially greater.

not recommended

Most building and demolition waste used to be dumped. In view of the environmental implications of landfill, it is recommendable to reduce dumping and to recycle waste.

basic selection

The separation of clean rubble, lowgrade chemical waste, metals, wood, synthetic materials and a residual fraction is generally considered to be a low-cost option.
The fraction of each type can be adjusted depending on the project's predicted waste flows. A fraction of glass, for instance, could be added when single glazing is replaced with double glazing.

97

comments

Separation of waste on building sites is to be preferred because tackling problems at source is best. Waste processing firms may prefer their consignments unsorted and to separate the waste themselves. This form of separating waste is appropriate for inner-city locations where space is at a premium.
A disadvantage, however, is that building site personnel are not directly involved.
The diagram below describes the principal reprocessing options for each type of waste. The alternative with the lowest number is practically feasible and this is the preferred choice from an environmental point of view.

waste types	processing method	primary reuse	secondary reuse	incineration	landfill
stone type materials		1	2		3
reinforced concrete			1		2
wood		1	2	3	4
synthetics			1	2	3
metals		1	2	3	4
paper and cardboard			1	2	3
glass		1	2		3
lowgrade chemical waste			1	2	3
other (e.g. domestic) waste			1	2	3

Wood preservation

preference 1	preference 2	preference 3	not recommended
avoid	localised	overall	—

environmental preference

Wood needs to be preserved when there is a threat of decay. (Note: insect damage is not a general problem in the Netherlands, and is therefore not yet considered as a factor in this environmental assessment.) Preservation can often be completely dispensed with, provided that the building element is well specified, a high-quality durable wood (properly seasoned and without knots) is used and that a protective finish is applied and well maintained.

A localised wood preservative in the form of a solid implant is preferred in some cases. Solid implants are inserted into the corner joints of window and door frames, for instance, as these are the most vulnerable locations. Expert opinion as to the efficiency of this measure varies considerably.

Overall preservation of wood is hardly ever necessary, nor is it desirable from an environmental point of view.

basic selection

Not given because this depends on the situation. See the respective building elements.

Localised preservation (solid implants)

preference 1	preference 2	preference 3	not recommended
borates	—	—	bifluoride, TBTO

environmental preference

A solid implant, based on borates, has been on the market for some time. This implant is only minimally harmful, degrades well and no noxious substances are released when the wood is burnt. Such implants have the additional advantage that preservation is localised, and as this is a dry implant, the active substances are only released when the degree of moisture reaches 20%, which reduces leaching. The pill remains effective for 5–10 years.

not recommended

Both the dry bifluoride (BF) implant and the liquid pill, based on TBTO (tributyl tin oxide), contain substances which are relatively toxic to the environment.

basic selection

Implants based on borates have been used in many projects and are listed in the basic selection on account of their minimal threat to the environment.

comments

Long-term experience has shown solid implants based on borates to be effective, provided that they contain diffusable preservatives.

Overall preservation

preference 1	*preference 2*	*preference 3*	*not recommended*
borates	quaternary ammonium compounds, zinc soaps, azoles	CCB salts, ZCF salts	CCA salts, improsol (BF) creosote oil

environmental preference

Borates are considerably less harmful to people and the environment than other preservatives. The disadvantage is that they leach in water. While this is not normally an issue, as they are generally in internal or protected situations, it can become a problem where the wood is in contact with the soil (in the case of a garden fence, for example). This can be combated by combining the borates with a natural preservative which renders the wood water-repellent. Natural preservative has no fungicidal effect. If this is not sufficient, then fixed preservatives such as quaternary ammonium compounds, zinc soaps and azoles can be used..

Preservative salts consist of a mixture of mainly heavy metals. CCA (copper chrome arsenic) salts are commonly used salts; their chromium and arsenic content is particularly harmful, though copper, which is responsible for the green colour, is much less harmful. CCB (chromium copper boron) and ZCF (zinc copper fluoride) salts contain fewer harmful elements than the CCA salts. Another important aspect is the ratio of the compounds in the preservative, which to a large extent determines the degree of leaching. Type B CCA salts leach more than type C CCA salts; they are therefore more environmentally damaging.

not recommended

CCA salts are not recommended on account of the presence of chromium and arsenic. Other harmful and poorly degradable preservatives are creosote oil and preservatives based on fluorides and tin oxide. The commonly used improsolates are an example of a preservative based on bifluoride.

basic selection

Quaternary ammonium compounds, zinc soaps and azoles are included in the basic selection but only when overall preservation is required.

comments

It is important for overall preservation to be done by firms holding a suitable quality assurance certificate. This ensures the stipulations on the preservative, the application method (high-pressure vacuum in a closed system) and its use (i.e. in contact with the soil or not) are adhered to.

99

Hard paving

preference 1	*preference 2*	*preference 3*	*not recommended*
recycled concrete slabs	concrete slabs, semi-open pavement	ceramic and concrete clinkers	asphalt

environmental preference

In general, restricting the extent of paving and aiming for water-permeable hardening is preferable from an environmental point of view. It enlarges the water collecting area, which favours the micro-climate. It reduces the burden on the water treatment plant , which helps to prevent annual overflows. Pilot studies already carried out, which have taken this into consideration, prove that a reduction of the hardening, including roof surfaces, from about 50% down to 40%, is feasible.
Recycled concrete slabs are preferable for paving as they consist partly of secondary raw materials. Slabs are generally preferable to clinkers due to their lower energy content. Grass turf has a limited use because of its structure, but it has the advantage of a smaller amount of material and greater water permeability.

not recommended

The use of asphalt in residential environments can be avoided. The environmental problems of asphalt are the extraction of limestone and gravel, emissions of SO_2, NO_2 and volatile organic compounds (phenols amongst others) in the production and processing and the release of small amounts of polycyclic aromatic hydrocarbons (PAHs) and asphalt fumes in processing (working conditions).

basic selection

Semi-open pavement is included in the basic selection. The basic choice for continuous paving is recycled concrete slabs because availability is no longer a problem. We expect that the price will no longer remain an obstacle either, in view of the large supply of concrete, brick or stone waste.

Semi-hard paving

preference 1	*preference 2*	*preference 3*	*not recommended*
wood chippings	sand	shells	gravel

environmental preference

Wood chippings are the most appropriate medium for semi-hard paths. The chippings are made by shredding branches and other prunings. A footpath needs additional new material after about four years, however.
Sand is slightly less desirable in comparison as the extraction carries consequences for the landscape and ecosystems.
Shells are admittedly a renewable raw material, but the rate of regeneration is too slow for large-scale use.

not recommended   The use of gravel for semi-hard paths is not recommended because the extraction of gravel affects the landscape. Better, less environmentally damaging alternatives are available for hardening paths.

basic selection   Shells are included in the basic selection for semi-hard paths, but wood chippings are an extremely good alternative, being easily available and cost effective.

For paving see 15

Garden partitioning

preference 1	preference 2	preference 3	not recommended
hedges	cuttings and pruning waste	untreated wood	recycled PVC, tropical wood, preserved wood

environmental preference

The use of hedges as garden partitioning contributes positively to the living environment. The urban micro climate (moisture control) is improved and nesting opportunities for various types of animals are increased. Many native shrubs are suitable for this purpose, depending on the soil. Some well-known examples are privet or hornbeam, blackthorn and hawthorn.

Partitions of cuttings and pruning waste consist of wood trimmings which have been woven. The trimmings are a waste product which is put to good use. It is debatable whether a partition made of untreated wood posts is a good idea because experience shows that many occupants remove and replace the existing partition when laying out a garden.

not recommended

The use of non-sustainable wood is not recommended, due to the effects on the ecosystems. Treated wood is not recommended on account of leaching preservatives, nor is recycled PVC posts. The use of synthetic waste for the production of garden fixtures and fittings is a form of reuse, but an important disadvantage is that it concerns a low-grade application. The use of such products is really dumping in disguise. PVC is stored, albeit usefully, before it actually ends up as landfill or in the incinerator. Ignorance about the life span of a garden also plays a part, and the risk of premature dumping or incineration is great.
If posts are used for fencing, then the omission of steel wires should be considered. They can harm the environment because of their heavy galvanisation and their short life span. Hemp rope should be considered if such a form of demarcation is desired.

basic selection

Untreated softwood posts, possibly combined with hemp rope, are cheaper and usually functional.

Privacy screens

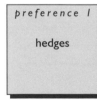

preference 1	preference 2	preference 3	not recommended
hedges	sustainable durable wood	masonry	tropical wood, preserved wood

environmental preference

See also *garden partitioning*. A privacy screen is normally expected to last longer than a garden partition. We have therefore ranked durable wood and masonry as second and third choices.

Masonry is more or less harmful to the environment depending on which block type is used.
See Appendix 1 for a more detailed description of the environmental impact of the materials mentioned.

not recommended

See *garden partitioning*.

basic selection

A masonry privacy screen is included in the basic selection; it is more expensive than the alternatives. The first and second preferences are cheaper alternatives.

comments

A wooden privacy screen should be prevented from coming into contact with damp soil by providing the posts with a concrete footing.

Outside storage

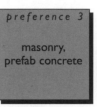

preference 1 — sustainable durable wood

preference 2 — painted softwood

preference 3 — masonry, prefab concrete

not recommended — tropical hardwood, preserved wood

environmental preference

See also *garden partitioning*. This application demands a long life-span, which is why hardwood is preferable, unless the wood is to be painted.
A painted shed made of softwood has the disadvantage that it must be painted regularly during the period in use. Boiled paint (see Appendix 1) is preferable to conventional paints for this application, as the paint is less harmful and the quantity required for painting is less. Boiled paint can be applied less frequently.
A masonry or prefabricated concrete shed is more environmentally damaging on account of the quantity and type of raw materials used, but it has the advantage of a longer life-span. A prefabricated concrete shed is also simple to dismantle and reassemble.
See Appendix 1 for a more detailed description of the environmental impact of the materials mentioned.

not recommended

See *garden partitioning*.

basic selection

A masonry or prefabricated concrete shed is included in the basic selection. A shed made from prefabricated concrete is no more expensive than treated wood.
A masonry shed is more costly.

comments

The preferences given in categories 21–25 *roof construction* also apply to the roof of the shed.

Combating rising damp

preference 1	*preference 2*	*preference 3*	*not recommended*
application of vapour barrier	injection with mineral	covering foundations with EPDM, tanking	covering foundations with bitumen, epoxy resin injection

environmental preference

Rising damp can be prevented by means of a damp-proof course immediately below the floor construction. Another way to prevent damp reaching the foundations is to fill them up by injection. Capillary paths can be interrupted by inserting a waterproof layer in the brickwork. This can be done with a polyethylene (PE) sheet membrane and concrete wedges, copper plates, a lead apron, or by pressing small, grooved, chrome-steel plates into the mortar. These materials are easily separated from the brickwork during demolition. PE membrane is the least environmentally damaging, followed by copper plates.

A mineral injection inserts a waterproof layer into the brickwork by filling up the capillaries over a certain course. The mineral injection does not contaminate the brickwork greatly.

An advantage of filling the foundations is that damp cannot penetrate the masonry; a disadvantage is that no moisture can leave it either, so that rainwater which has leached down the facade cannot leave it. Injecting foundations uses a lot of material, compared with the other variants.

not recommended

The use of epoxy resin, or bitumen, for injections leads to contaminated masonry in the demolition phase. Moreover, harmful substances are released during the production and injection of epoxy resin. The manufacture of bituminous products causes considerable pollution, from the extraction of petroleum via refining up to and including waste disposal.

basic selection

The solution is heavily dependent on the circumstances. A basic selection is therefore not included.

comments

If rising damp does not cause much trouble, then a solution might be to incorporate some drainage around the facade. This could be done in the form of a gravel bed, through which the moisture can drain quickly, or by laying drains.

A correct diagnosis is paramount where damp is concerned. Covering the soil and inserting a damp-proof course into the foundation does not necessarily solve dampness problems. Inserting a damp-proof course into the walls is not a simple task, and it is expensive.

21–25 Floor construction

For floor screeds see 42
For insulation ground floor see 37

Ground floors

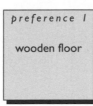

preference 1	preference 2	preference 3	not recommended
wooden floor	hollow concrete elements (joists/fillers)	—	concrete (solid)

environmental preference

Wood is the first choice for replacing an existing wooden floor, provided the ground under the suspended floor permits this (damp, dirt). Wooden ground floors must be made reasonably airtight, due to radon and the transfer of moisture from the ground under the suspended floor to the space above.

Less material is needed for a wooden floor than for a floor made of concrete joists, fillers or hollow elements. Wood is a renewable material whereas the raw materials needed for concrete are scarce and their extraction often affects the landscape. A wooden floor also causes fewer problems for waste disposal than a concrete floor.

See Part 4 for a more detailed description of the environmental impact of the materials mentioned.

not recommended

Solid concrete uses more material than hollow structures.

basic selection

Wooden floor.

comments

Sealing the space under the suspended floor or making the ground floor airtight is labour-intensive, which also makes such operations expensive.

The application of a floor made from concrete joists and fillers should be considered in certain situations where damp poses a significant threat.

107

Balconies

preference 1	preference 2	preference 3	not recommended
sustainable durable wood elements	sectional steel, aluminium	—	ferro cement, tropical wood

environmental preference

Balconies are generally badly affected by moisture, which demands the use of a durable material. Wood with a Class II durability rating does not need to be treated when used externally. Wood is a renewable material and degrades well in the decomposition phase. Sectional steel and aluminium elements can be reused at a later stage, but steel must be treated to prevent corrosion. The extraction and production of aluminium is harmful to the environment, particularly because its high energy content. Aluminium, like steel, is eminently reusable.

See Part 4 for a more detailed description of the environmental impact of the materials mentioned.

not recommended

The use of non-sustainable wood is not recommended on account of the damage to the ecosystem.
Ferro-cement balcony sheets are filled with a synthetic foam to keep their weight down. This creates a composite material which impedes the reuse of the materials in the waste phase.

basic selection

Sectional steel and aluminium.

21–25 Internal wall construction

For damp-proofing see 20
For non-solid internal walls see 44

Internal walls

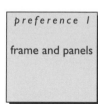

preference 1

frame and panels

preference 2

solid

preference 3

—

not recommended

—

environmental preference

An internal wall consisting of a frame with panels has the advantage that less material is needed than for solid walls. A cavity wall is also relatively simple to remove. Less waste will be produced when changing the layout of the house.
As a building method it is eminently suited to refurbishment. No wet materials are involved (no mortar or adhesives, less nuisance) and the materials are light.
A choice of solid concrete, stone or brick for internal walls is more obvious for construction methods using concrete, stone or brick.

basic selection

No basic selection is included as this depends on the method of building and the functional demands specified.

comments

An internal wall consisting of a frame with panels has little mass and therefore minimal sound insulation. To achieve good sound insulation in dwellings, terraced houses and town houses the wall should be flexibly anchored to the floor and a properly continuous insulation layer should be applied.
Attaching objects to wall panels is less simple for the occupants. Special plugs have to be used.

109

Solid internal walls

preference 1

loam construction

preference 2

flue-gas gypsum blocks, sand-lime blocks

preference 3

cellular concrete blocks, natural gypsum blocks

not recommended

—

environmental preference

Loam consists of a mixture of clay and sand, and possibly straw. Loam construction is unusual on account of its labour-intensive character, but it has many environmental advantages: it consumes no scarce raw materials, the production process is not harmful and it has a very low energy content.
An internal wall of sand-lime-blocks has the advantage that the raw materials are plentiful, the production demands little energy and is relatively clean. Concrete blockwork is made from gypsum, a by-product from electricity power plants, which counts in its favour.
Cellular concrete has the disadvantage that the required raw materials are scarce and that the energy consumption during production is rather high. Natural gypsum scores less well than gypsum from power plants, due to the impact its extraction has on the landscape.
See Part 4 for a more detailed description of the environmental impact of the materials mentioned.

basic selection

comments

Flue-gas gypsum blocks are now freely available and can be used at low cost.

The junction of solid internal walls to load-bearing walls and ceilings requires special consideration. Gypsum blocks generally involve the use of PVC mouldings which seal the gap visually. This can be avoided by using elastic tape and joinery.
There is little difference in price between the materials mentioned. Producers of natural gypsum blocks and board are in the process of changing over to gypsum recovered from power plants. This is very attractive in view of the problems with the extraction of natural gypsum, particularly in Germany.

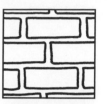

21–25 External wall construction

For insulation following building completion see 37
For external wall plasterwork see 40
For external wall claddings see 31

External walls

preference 1	*preference 2*	*preference 3*	*not recommended*
repointing	application of durable wood, sustainable multi-ply	application of mineral render	application of synthetic render

environmental preference

Repointing with a mortar is preferable to adding an external wall cladding or render, because less material is used. The durability of the newly pointed brickwork is greater than that of the other options.
Adding an external wall cladding made of durable wood or plywood made of non-tropical woods is preferable to render, because render generally requires more maintenance.
Mineral render contains considerably less synthetics than a synthetic-based render. Another advantage of mineral render is that less maintenance is needed.

not recommended

Synthetic render contains about 10% synthetics. This mixture of synthetics with concrete, stone or brick contaminates the building and demolition waste.

basic selection

Not included, as this depends on the circumstances.

comments

We assume that the addition of insulation is to the exterior wall skin. The place of application depends on the construction of the external wall and this will be dealt with below. The repair work referred to above must be seen in context with the insulation method.
Colouring the mineral render with the aid of an additive reduces maintenance, as there is no need to repaint.

111

Cleaning external walls

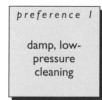

preference 1	*preference 2*	*preference 3*	*not recommended*
damp, low-pressure cleaning	dry, low-pressure cleaning	wet, high-pressure cleaning	chemical cleaning

environmental preference

Cleaning concrete and masonry with the aid of water or grit jets is a mechanical method which does not require aggressive chemicals. These less environmentally damaging cleaning techniques have been developed over the years and the end results are as good as those of the other options.
High-pressure cleaning sprays dirt, sand or metal particles into the air, which can be damaging to the health of unprotected bystanders.
Low-pressure jets consisting of damp grit prevents the dispersion of dust particles into the air. Another advantage of low-pressure jets compared with high-pressure jets is that the surface to be cleaned is damaged less and its life-span is therefore increased.

not recommended

The use of a lot of water (with or without steel grit) contaminates the soil with waste material. Catching the contaminated grit is simple with a damp system. Systems which reuse this grit after cleaning are preferred.

basic selection

Cleaning concrete and masonry with the aid of chemicals (bases, acids, organic solvents) is not recommended as there are adequate alternatives.

Damp-cleaning under low pressure.

comments

No cleaning is the preferred option from an environmental point of view. However, cleaning can improve the look of a building and so contribute to an improvement in the living environment. Repairs to concrete and masonry often make cleaning inevitable, and before an external wall can be water-proofed, it has to be cleaned.
Chemical cleansing, sand jets and high-pressure jets are prohibited by many local authorities and the use of other methods is often subject to restrictions. It is important for the work to be screened off and leakage to the soil to be prevented.

Damming external walls

preference 1

water-based system

preference 2

—

preference 3

—

not recommended

solvent-based system

environmental preference

Moisture permeation can be prevented by waterproofing. Waterproofing is a water-repellent treatment where the pores of the stones are made water-repellent although the external wall remains moisture permeable. The transport of moisture from inside to the outside remains possible, but water can no longer penetrate the external wall. The production process and the use of water-based water-repellents are less environmentally damaging than alternatives based on solvents.
See Part 4 for a more detailed description of the environmental impact of the materials mentioned.

not recommended

The use of organic solvent-based waterproofing is not recommended.

basic selection

Waterproofing with a water-based repellent.

comments

Masonry must be repaired and cleaned before an external wall can be waterproofed. The water-proofing medium must be applied with care and in accordance with the supplier's instructions. There is a danger that the permeability of moisture from the inside could become quite bad, creating damp and mould problems on the inside of the wall.

Repairing concrete

preference 1	*preference 2*	*preference 3*	*not recommended*
mineral filler	—	—	epoxy-resin filler

Concrete surfacing

preference 1	*preference 2*	*preference 3*	*not recommended*
mineral coating	water-based coating	—	other coating

environmental preference

The production process of mineral concrete filler and mineral coating is less polluting than that of fillers and coatings based on epoxy resin. Mineral products cause fewer problems for waste disposal too, because they contaminate the concrete less and are more degradable.

A mineral material with a different composition can be used for a smooth finish of the concrete surface. A disadvantage of applying a surface is that a new coat must be applied regularly.

not recommended

The use of epoxy resin causes the concrete to be contaminated in the waste stage and it is therefore less suitable for reuse in the form of reclaimed aggregate. In addition the production and use of epoxy resin-based materials releases harmful substances.

basic selection

Mineral materials for repair and surfaces have been included in the basic selection.

comments

Mineral-based concrete fillers and surfaces cost about the same as those based on epoxy resin.

113

21–25 Roof construction

For roof coverings see 33
For insulation of existing roofs see 37

Pitched roof construction

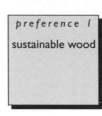

preference 1	*preference 2*	*preference 3*	*not recommended*
sustainable wood	box panels, sustainable plywood, chipboard (<2mg formaldehyde)	chipboard	plywood made from tropical wood

environmental preference

A traditional roof construction of softwood purlins with a softwood roof covering is preferable. Softwood panels do not contain environmentally-damaging adhesives, in contrast to plywood. OSB and chipboard common box panels are fast to work with on site and have the environmental advantage that it is possible to use cellulose for insulation. It must however be a box with an OSB finish or plywood finish not made of tropical woods, e.g. Oregon pine. Currently a new type of chipboard with less than 2 mg of formaldehyde per kg has been developed.

Roof elements with the insulation layer bonded to the panels have the disadvantage that the various components can barely be separated following demolition. A loose or mechanically fixed insulation layer is therefore preferred in all cases.

See Part 4 for a more detailed description of the environmental impact of the materials mentioned.

not recommended

Plywood sheets made from tropical woods are not recommended on account of the depletion of tropical rain forests.

basic selection

Roof covering made from plywood sheets containing non-tropical woods, e.g. Oregon pine, is included in the basic selection. It is already a much-used product in current construction practice.

comments

The fixing of softwood elements is more labour-intensive, which makes the cost higher than for sheet materials. A box panel (with a filling of mineral wool) is 10%–20% cheaper than the other variants. A filling of cellulose on the other hand is a little more expensive.

Flat roof construction

preference 1	*preference 2*	*preference 3*	*not recommended*
softwood rafters and roof coverings	steel sheets	—	roof battens of plywood made from tropical wood

environmental preference

A traditional roof construction of softwood rafters with a softwood covering is also preferable for flat roofs. Softwood panels do not contain environmentally harmful adhesives, in contrast to plywood.

Profiled steel plates can be used for flat roofs, which stretch from load-bearing wall to load-bearing wall, without any support structure below. The steel plate is extremely thin (e.g. only 0.88 mm) which limits the amount of material. A disadvantage is the galvanised thermal layer, which is indispensable to prevent corrosion.

See Part 4 for a more detailed description of the environmental impact of the materials mentioned.

not recommended

Plywood sheets made from tropical hardwoods are not recommended due to the depletion of tropical rain forests.

basic selection

Steel roof plates have been included in the basic selection.

comments

The fitting of softwood panels is more labour intensive, which makes the cost higher than that of the alternatives.

Flashings

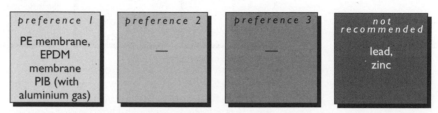

preference 1	preference 2	preference 3	not recommended
PE membrane, EPDM membrane PIB (with aluminium gas)	—	—	lead, zinc

environmental preference

Polyethylene (PE) and ethylene propylene diene monomer (EPDM) membranes are more durable than zinc. PE, EPDM, bitumen and polyisobutene (PIB) are less harmful and more readily available alternatives to lead and zinc.
See Part 4 for a more detailed description of the environmental impact of the materials mentioned.

not recommended

Lead is extremely harmful to human health. Lead enters the environment during its use as lead flashings and later during the decomposition stage.
Used zinc is not recommended as corrosion can lead to the contamination of wastewater or soil with consequent damage to many organisms. Zinc is also a scarce resource with a relatively short life.

basic selection

PE and EPDM membranes can be used around frames and for filling internal cavity wall panels. As the use of lead cannot be avoided in all cases we have not included this unit in the basic selection.

comments

When PE and EPDM membranes are used for the junction then these membranes must be prevented from blowing off in the wind. The use of lead proves to be inevitable in certain situations, such as at the junction of a tiled roof with rising brickwork. These membranes are about 20% more expensive than zinc and lead.

30 External window frames and doors

For preservative treatments see 06
For glazing see 34
For paintwork see 46

Frame refurbishment

preference 1	preference 2	preference 3	not recommended
repair	replacement or repair	—	total replacement

environmental preference

Frame repair is less environmentally damaging than replacement with new frames when the existing frames are not seriously damaged. If the frames are in a bad condition, then the pollution from the repairs can be greater, as there is not much difference in the amount of material needed for repair and replacement, and repaired frames require more maintenance than new frames. A combination of repairing frames in a reasonable condition and replacing frames which are in bad condition is preferable to replacing all damaged frames.

not recommended

Total replacement of all the frames, regardless, is not recommended as there are no sound technical reasons for doing this.

basic selection

Replacement/repair is included in the basic selection. Maintenance supplemented with repair is a good structural approach for frames, once a particular quality is present. This saves money in the end, as replacement will no longer be necessary. In contrast to frames, windows cannot or can hardly be restored.

comments

The glazing groove in existing frames may be unsuitable for the application of insulating glazing. This can be resolved by installing double window frames (see 34 *glazing*).

116

Repairing frames

preference 1	preference 2	preference 3	not recommended
insert piece of sustainable wood with epoxy resin	—	insert piece of softwood with epoxy resin and borate	insert piece of tropical wood with polyester, BF or TBTO pill

environmental preference

Replacing the damaged wooden parts with softwood made to measure by sawing and milling is the least environmentally damaging alternative. The use of epoxy resin as a filler and for attaching material is necessary for reasons of durability.
The use of preservatives is superfluous when the repair is combined with careful reglazing, paintwork and maintenance.
If preservation is used anyway for peace of mind, then this is best done locally with borate-based materials. There is no need to treat the whole frame as damage to the frame nearly always occurs at the joints.
See Part 4 for a more detailed description of the environmental impact of the materials mentioned.

not recommended	The use of non-sustainable wood is not recommended on account of the depletion of the ecosystem. Softwood is satisfactory when repairs are done well. The threat of polyester and epoxy resin is of the same order, but a repair done with epoxy resin lasts considerably longer. The use of BF and TBTO pills must be avoided in view of the damaging effects of tin oxides and, to a lesser extent, bifluorides.
basic selection	The insertion of a piece of non-tropical wood with epoxy resin.
comments	In practice the replacement of damaged sections of wood is combined with drilling out less serious damage, and filling with resin. Filling is possible to a maximum of 10cm^3 for reasons of durability. Epoxy resin, prior to hardening, contains substances which are extremely harmful to the person handling it. It is important that protective measures are taken.

External window frames

preference 1	*preference 2*	*preference 3*	*not recommended*
sustainable durable wood, untreated softwood	softwood with solid borate implant	aluminium, preserved softwood, recycled PVC	tropical wood, PVC

environmental preference

The production process of an aluminium or PVC frame is much more environmentally damaging than that of a wooden frame. Recycled PVC means a substantial fraction has been recycled. Alternatively, future recycling should be guaranteed. Poor quality softwood, requiring large amounts of preservative, was much used in the 1960s and 70s, and softwood gained a poor reputation. Today, though softwood frames are often of high quality, the practice of using large amounts of preservative remains, resulting in much 'over' preserved softwood. The use of more durable woods is one possible solution. Untreated softwood frames are also a possible solution, provided that the quality of the selected wood, the specification and finish has received sufficient attention for their durability to be about the same as that of treated frames.
See Part 4 for a more detailed description of the environmental impact of the materials mentioned.

not recommended

Use of non-sustainable wood is not recommended due to the depletion of the ecosystem.

basic selection

Softwood treated with solid borate implants.

comments

The untreated softwood frames mentioned under environmental preference are supplied with a guarantee of 10 years. These frames are however more expensive than the alternatives. The price of frames varies with the area. Aluminium frames are nearly always the most expensive. An advantage of aluminium frames is that an extremely high-grade reuse is possible.

External doors

preference 1	*preference 2*	*preference 3*	*not recommended*
sustainable durable wood, untreated softwood	softwood with solid borate implant, sustainable multi-ply	aluminium, preserved softwood, recycled PVC	tropical wood, PVC

environmental preference

A factor to be taken into account is that wooden external doors may be treated with harmful preservatives in order to prevent wood decay when damp. A less environmentally damaging variant is the use of more durable woods. Untreated softwood doors, in which the quality of the wood, the specification and finish have been carefully safeguarded, are also satisfactory. A plywood door is an alternative choice. A disadvantage with plywood is the use of adhesives which can be harmful to the environment.

The production process of a wooden external door is much less environmentally damaging than that of an aluminium or PVC external door.

An advantage with aluminium doors is the possibility of high-grade recycling compared with PVC doors. 'Recycled PVC' means that a substantial fraction has been recycled. Alternatively, future recycling should be guaranteed.

Balcony and access doors are often protected against damp by overhanging balconies or galleries, and by entrances or awnings. Untreated pine or room doors can be used satisfactorily here.

See Part 4 for a more detailed description of the environmental impact of the materials mentioned.

not recommended

The use of non-sustainable wood is not recommended on account of the depletion of the ecosystem. Plywood should not be made of tropical wood.

basic selection

An external door made of plywood or softwood, possibly with a borax pill, is included in the basic selection as these are common types of doors.

30 Internal window frames and doors

For glazing see 34
For paintwork see 46

Internal window frames

preference 1	*preference 2*	*preference 3*	*not recommended*
sustainable wood	galvanised and coated steel	—	tropical wood

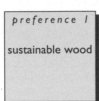  

environmental preference

The production process of a steel frame is more environmentally damaging than that of a softwood frame. Wooden frames are preferable, despite the larger quantity of material. See Part 4 for a more detailed description of the environmental impact of the materials mentioned.

not recommended

The use of non-sustainable wood is not recommended on account of the depletion of the ecosystem.

basic selection

Softwood internal frames.

comments

Softwood internal frames are usually slightly cheaper than steel frames, but the difference in cost depends on the method of construction.

119

Internal doors

preference 1	*preference 2*	*preference 3*	*not recommended*
honeycomb with hardboard skins	European softwood	sustainable plywood, chipboard	tropical wood

environmental preference

Plasterboard pollutes more than softwood. The amount of material needed for a honeycomb door with hardboard skin is much smaller, and this is the reason for preferring this door. The production process of an aluminium or steel door causes considerably more pollution than that of an untreated softwood internal door. Chipboard internal doors are faced with a synthetic layer (melamine) which impedes efficient processing of waste.

not recommended

See Part 4 for a more detailed description of the environmental impact of the materials mentioned.

basic selection

The use of non-sustainable wood is not recommended on account of the depletion of the ecosystem. Honeycomb door with hardboard skins.

comments

The honeycomb door with hardboard skins is cheapest.

Internal door thresholds

preference 1	preference 2	preference 3	not recommended
sustainable durable wood	sustainable softwood	steel with coating	tropical wood

environmental preference

The production process of steel thresholds is considerably more harmful to the environment than that of wooden thresholds. Hardwoods are preferred as they stand up better against wear and tear. Thresholds made from European deciduous trees have a longer life-span than those made from softwood.
See Part 4 for a more detailed description of the environmental impact of the materials mentioned.

not recommended

The use of non-sustainable hardwood is not recommended on account of the depletion of the ecosystem.

basic selection

Sustainable durable wood. In particular, thresholds made of beech are already widely used, except in wet environments.

Window sills

preference 1	preference 2	preference 3	not recommended
ceramic tiles, solid natural stone, softwood	sustainable plywood, manufactured stone	fibre cement, chipboard, synthetic stone	—

environmental preference

The production processes of fibre cement, chipboard and synthetic stone window sills cause worse pollution than those of stone-like materials and of wood. An asset of wood (also the raw material for plywood) is that it is a renewable raw material. A wooden window sill still requires surface treatment.
Chipboard and synthetic stone have a larger amount of harmful adhesive than plywood or manufactured (cast) stone. The adhesive can cause problems during production, during occupation and as waste material. Synthetic stone is more polluting than manufactured stone, due to the use of bonding agents. Chipboard window sills are faced with a synthetic layer (melamine) which complicates efficient waste processing.
See Part 4 for a more detailed description of the environmental impact of the materials mentioned.

basic selection

Sustainable plywood.

comments

Tiles are less suitable than wood in certain situations, e.g. in the case of a wooden wall panel. A window sill of tiles is the cheapest, followed by a window sill of chipboard or solid softwood. Solid softwood, however, requires more maintenance.

External wall cladding

preference 1	*preference 2*	*preference 3*	*not recommended*
sustainable durable wood	sustainable plywood, synthetic resin-bonded (wood-fibre) board	fibre-cement board, synthetic resin bonded (paper) board	tropical wood, steel

environmental preference

Wood is renewable and degrades easily, an advantage over fibre cement and synthetic resin board. Wood preservation and paintwork can be dispensed with if durable woods are used. This causes less pollution and requires less maintenance during occupation. The objection to plywood and synthetic resin board lies in the bonding agents used (synthetic resins), the production of which harms the environment. The percentage of bonding agents in synthetic resin boards is, at about 30%, higher than in plywood, which is at about 5%, and additional energy is required for its production. The harm to the environment resulting from maintenance (varnish, paint) and the quality and quantity of wood required for the veneers puts plywood at a disadvantage. Wood produced from thinning, remnants and recycled sheet material, can be used for synthetic resin board based on wood fibres, but only paper can be used in the production of synthetic resin board based on paper laminate. Using recycled board material is not an option.
Cement is the bonding agent used in cement fibreboard. It has the drawback that the raw materials are scarce. Its other drawbacks, compared with other boards, are increased weight per square metre and greater vulnerability.
See Part 4 for a more detailed description of the environmental impact of the materials mentioned.

not recommended

The use of non-sustainable wood is not recommended on account of the depletion of the ecosystem. The extraction of coal (coke) and iron ore for steel and the production of steel results in considerable damage to the environment. Steel has been put in the 'not recommended' category because sufficient alternatives are available.

basic selection

Fibre cement and synthetic resin bonded sheets are included in the basic selection.

comments

Untreated durable woods become grey over the years because they are affected by the weather. The greying has no deleterious effect on the quality of the wood. Cladding with durable wood or plywood is the cheapest solution, but plywood must be regularly maintained. The cost of synthetic fibre bonded sheets is highest; however, they have the advantage of requiring hardly any maintenance.

121

Internal stairs

preference 1	*preference 2*	*preference 3*	*not recommended*
European wood	—	steel	tropical wood

environmental preference

A softwood staircase is the preferred choice; a disadvantage of these staircases is the phenol-content of the bonding in laminated sustainable wood strings. Direct reuse is no problem with wooden and steel stairs. A sectional construction is preferred in all cases with regard to recycling. Steel as a material is problematic in view of the extraction of the raw materials, coal and iron ore, and the pollution caused in manufacture. Steel has a high energy content.
See Part 4 for a more detailed description of the environmental impact of the materials mentioned.

not recommended

The use of non-sustainable wood is not recommended on account of the depletion of the ecosystems.

basic selection

An internal staircase of European softwood is commonly used and cheap, and has therefore been included in the basic selection.

122

comments

A softwood staircase is by far the cheapest of the alternatives mentioned. Different demands, relating to fire safety amongst other things, are made on a staircase which is common to several dwellings, than on an internal staircase within one dwelling.

External stairs

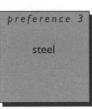

preference 1	*preference 2*	*preference 3*	*not recommended*
sustainable durable wood	—	steel	tropical wood, preserved wood

environmental preference

An external staircase of durable wood is preferable because the material is renewable. Recycling offers no problems for steel and wooden stairs. Sectional attachment is preferable. The choice of steel or concrete is in practice based on functional and aesthetic demands. Steel is used for fire escapes, in particular.
See Part 4 for a more detailed description of the environmental impact of the materials mentioned.

not recommended

The use of non-sustainable wood is not recommended on account of its impact on ecosystems. Wood preservatives should be avoided due to the leaching of harmful substances.

basic selection

Steel, as wooden external stairs are not always suitable.

| comments | Fire regulations can prevent the use of wooden external stairs in certain cases. Wooden stairs are more expensive than steel ones due to the higher cost of durable woods and the lack of mass production. |

Internal balustrades/railings

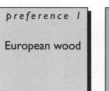 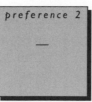  

preference 1	*preference 2*	*preference 3*	*not recommended*
European wood	—	steel	tropical wood

environmental preference

Sustainable European softwood is preferable to steel for internal balustrades and rails. Steel is problematic due to the extraction of coal and iron ore and to pollution occurring during manufacture.
See Part 4 for a more detailed description of the environmental impact of the materials mentioned.

not recommended

The use of non-sustainable wood for balustrades and railings is not recommended on account of its impact on ecosystems.

basic selection

European wood is acceptable and cheap.

comments

Beech is a good choice for railings because it is flexible and hard. The price of beech railing is comparable to that of hardwood railing. Softwood balustrades are a little cheaper than balustrades made of meranti or merbau.
Steel stair-gates are dearest.

123

External balustrades/railings

preference 1	*preference 2*	*preference 3*	*not recommended*
sustainable durable wood	—	steel, aluminium	tropical wood, preserved wood

environmental preference

Durable wood is preferable to steel for external balustrades and rails. Steel which is used externally must be treated to prevent corrosion. Sectional steel elements can be reused primarily at a later stage.
The extraction and manufacture of aluminium causes heavy pollution, particularly because of its high energy content. Aluminium, like steel, is eminently recyclable.
See Part 4 for a more detailed description of the environmental impact of the materials mentioned.

not recommended

The use of non-sustainable wood for balustrades and railings is not recommended on account of depletion of the ecosystem. The use of wood preservatives should also be avoided if possible.

basic selection

Steel or aluminium. Balustrades made of durable wood are an obvious choice when in combination with wooden stairs.

comments

Steel rails for an external staircase are somewhat cheaper than wooden rails.

Pitched roof coverings

preference 1	*preference 2*	*preference 3*	*not recommended*
timber shingles, reed	clay or concrete roof tiles	fibre-cement slates, corrugated panels, bituminous slates	zinc, copper

environmental preference

Timber shingles and reed are renewable, in contrast with the other options, and they are therefore the first choice for covering pitched roofs.

A preference for clay or concrete roof tiles cannot be expressed without further detailed research. The production of clay tiles requires a relatively large amount of energy. More harmful substances are emitted in their production, than during the manufacture of concrete tiles. The extraction of binding agents and the production of cement are the most environmentally damaging aspects of the manufacture of concrete tiles. The environmental effects of concrete and clay tiles balance each other out. Slates and corrugated sheets made of fibre cement contain more cement than do concrete tiles, and are less durable. Bituminous slates are a product of the petroleum processing industry. See Part 4 for a more detailed description of the environmental impact of the materials mentioned.

not recommended

Sufficient alternatives are available for a pitched roof to eliminate the need for zinc and copper. The corrosion of these can lead to contamination of water and soil, with consequent damage to organisms. In addition zinc is a relatively scarce resource with a short life.

basic selection

Clay and concrete tiles are common and are therefore included in the basic selection.

comments

Reeds, as well as timber shingles, can cause problems in urban areas due to their flammability. Their use is at present recommended only in detached situations.
Concrete tiles are by far the cheapest, followed by ceramic tiles and slates. Timber shingles are considerably more expensive.

Flat roof coverings

preference 1	preference 2	preference 3	not recommended
—	EPDM sheet, modified bitumen felt (APP, SBS)	blown bitumen felt, recycled PVC, EPDM with bitumen layer	zinc, PVC

Fixing coverings

preference 1	preference 2	preference 3	not recommended
loose with plants	loose with gravel or tiles	mechanical	glued, bonded

environmental preference

Repairing an old roof covering is preferable to replacement, but this depends on the quality of the old covering and its remaining life-span. A disadvantage with repairs is that the new material is bonded to the old, often with many layers of bitumen containing harmful polycyclic aromatic hydrocarbons (PAHs). The amount of contaminated demolition waste is therefore increased.

Ethylene propylene diene monomer (EPDM) is an elastomeric, synthetic sheet material which can easily be reused, primarily when it is loose or has been mechanically attached. EPDM is longer-lasting than roofing felt made with blown bitumen.
Atactic polypropylene (APP) and styrene-butadiene-styrene (SBS) bitumen are the materials most commonly used in the manufacture of roofing felts. APP bitumen consists of about 70% bitumen and 30% of APP. SBS bitumen consists of 87% bitumen and 13% SBS. APP bitumen is in itself resistant to ultra-violet radiation, but SBS bitumen requires a mineralised coating. Both materials have a considerably longer life-span (about 20 years) than the 'usual' blown bitumen. Modified bitumen systems have few layers and are thinner than blown bitumen. One-coating bitumen is also often not fixed, which simplifies reuse. The mixtures, consisting of a top layer of EPDM and a bitumen lower layer, cause problems during waste disposal, if glued or bonded. 'Recycled PVC' means that a substantial fraction has been recycled. Alternatively, future recycling should be guaranteed.

By ballasting or mechanically attaching a roof covering, rather than bonding it, we can increase the opportunities for recycling. Ballasting protects the roof covering against the effects of the weather and in particular against ultra-violet radiation, which lengthens its life-span. Ballasting with sedum plants on a base of clay granules is preferable in view of the scarcity of gravel. Sedum plants are a kind of succulent, relatively impervious to arid conditions. A green roof has a water buffer capacity (helping to avoid the overloading of sewers) and improves the micro-climate in towns (dust attraction, humidity control). See Part 4 for a more detailed description of the environmental impact of the materials mentioned.

not recommended

The durability and recycling opportunities of sheet PVC are greater than those of bitumen. The pollution caused through sheet PVC production and the processing of PVC waste is, however, so great that bitumen still wins out. The production of zinc is relatively harmful and the metal is scarce. A substantial fraction of PVC should be recycled, or future recycling guaranteed.
Glueing or bonding roofing materials has the result that the material can no longer, (or only with difficulty) be separated from the insulation or roof structure, which causes problems for waste disposal. The production and application of solvent-based adhesives impedes health, as well as the environment.

basic selection

EPDM, APP and SBS bituminous roof covering are included in the basic selection.

comments

The additional costs of EPDM are quite high. A disadvantage of a green roof is that the structure must have a larger load-bearing capacity. This must be taken into account in the case of wooden roofs.

34 Glazing

For sealants see 36
For window frames see 30

Glazing type

preference 1	preference 2	preference 3	not recommended
argon-filled LE-glazing	air-filled LE-glazing	double glazing	single glazing

environmental preference

By LE-glazing we mean glass with a low emissivity coating. LE-glazing (U=1.6) has a lower U-value than double glazing (U=3) and single glazing (U=5.7).
Argon-filled LE-glazing with a coating of silver insulates best (U=1.3). The energy-savings of this are so significant that they outweigh the environmental threat from the use of the cavity gas and coating. LE-glazing should be used as much as possible to achieve significant energy savings.

not recommended

The use of single glazing in domestic dwellings not recommended from the point of view of both energy saving and living comfort.

basic selection

LE-glazing for living rooms and double glazing for bedrooms.

comments

LE-glazing is at present still 25%–35% dearer than double-glazing. It is to be expected that the difference in price will decrease in view of the rapid increase in the use of LE-glazing. The introduction of an energy performance standard (EPN) for grading products will accelerate this.
Double glazing is more expensive than single glazing, particularly when the existing frames must be adapted. The additional costs of LE-glazing compared with double glazing are recovered by the savings made in its lifetime. An insulation subsidy for existing dwellings with separate levels in the subsidy sums given for double and LE-glazing could be made available. This is currently the case in the Netherlands.

127

Refurbishment approach

preference 1	preference 2	preference 3	not recommended
replacement with LE or double glazing	secondary glazing	—	single glazing

environmental preference

The frequent use of LE-glazing is necessary to achieve desirable energy savings. Existing frames may not be suitable for using double or LE-glazing, which might be a problem, but replacing frames for this reason would be undesirable (see 30 *window frames*). The problem can be resolved by installing secondary glazing and retaining the single-glazing so that the insulation value then becomes comparable with that of double-glazing. This saves material and energy compared with the replacement of frames with double-glazing.

not recommended

Single glass in dwellings is not recommended for reasons of energy saving and, to a lesser extent, living comfort.

basic selection

Secondary glazing is in the basic selection. The additional costs are considerably greater than with single glazing, but the energy savings are great.

comments

When new frames with double or LE-glazing are fitted into external walls consisting of stone masonry, then it is important that the nature of the wall, and the building's ventilation are considered, otherwise damp problems due to condensation may occur. Provided these points are considered, the replacement of frames and glazing will not only give energy savings, but will also improve living comfort.

Installing glazing

preference 1	*preference 2*	*preference 3*	*not recommended*
dry glazing	semi-dry glazing	wet glazing	—

environmental preference

Dry glazing with a rubber sealant is preferable to other methods on account of its greater durability. Wet glazing with sealant or putty requires more maintenance. The maintenance cycle for semi-dry glazing, which combines a rubber seal within the glass cavity with external wooden mouldings and sealant, lies between that of the other methods. Elastomeric sealants are preferable to plastic ones in view of the greater durability they achieve (see 36 *sealants*).

basic selection

Wet glazing (with elastomeric sealant) is recommended for existing frames, as dry glazing is not a simple operation with existing frames. Dry glazing is thoroughly recommended for new frames, although it is somewhat more expensive.

comments

Wooden mouldings are used in installing double and LE-glazing. They can have rubber seals and/or a sealant may be used. The material preference for the mouldings is similar to that of external frames and windows (see 30 *window frames*).

Thresholds

preference 1	preference 2	preference 3	not recommended
solid natural stone	ceramic tiles, manufactured stone	synthetic stone	—

environmental preference

Manufactured (cast) stone is more polluting than solid natural stone due to the use of bonding agents. The production of ceramic tiles uses more energy than the production of solid natural stone.
Synthetic stone is concrete which is not reinforced and to which double-figure percentages of polyester are added. The production process of polyester pollutes.

basic selection

Synthetic stone.

comments

A threshold made of tiles is much more expensive due to it being labour-intensive.
A solid natural stone threshold is a little more expensive than a synthetic stone threshold.

129

Sealing joints

preference 1	*preference 2*	*preference 3*	*not recommended*
coconut fibre, felt, sisal	mineral wool, PE tape, EPDM seal	elastomeric sealant with base filler	PUR foam, PUR sealant

environmental preference

Renewable raw materials such as coconut fibre and felt can be used for sealing joints. They are products which have been processed only minimally and are therefore less environmentally damaging.

As a second choice we list products which are produced from non-renewable raw materials, but which have a limited impact on the environment with regard to their extraction and manufacture: polyethylene (PE) foam tape on a roll, mineral wool bands and ethylene propylene diene monomer (EPDM) synthetic rubber seals. The production process of PE results in a greater threat to the environment than that of mineral wool. The important point is that PE is not foamed with chlorofluorocarbons (CFCs). The solution, in which an elastomeric sealant is applied to a base filling, requires more maintenance that the other variants. Large amounts of sealant are involved, depending on the width of the joint.

See Part 4 for a more detailed description of the environmental impact of the materials mentioned.

not recommended

The largest problem of polyurethane (PUR) foam is the propellant which is used for foaming. This uses CFCs which damage the ozone layer. At present other foaming agents, such as hydro-fluorocarbons, (H)CFCs, are often used, which are less of a threat to the ozone layer. The use of PUR sealant and PUR foam with an ozone-friendly foaming agent is not recommended, as a great many other deleterious substances are released in the production of PUR. Polyurethane foam has the additional disadvantage that the strong adhesion impedes the reuse of the materials.

basic selection

The sealant to be applied depends on the functional demands being made. In most cases materials from preference 2 will be satisfactory. These materials would have been included in the basic selection were it not for the fact that the use of PUR cannot always be excluded in practice.

comments

The use of sealants for joints can be reduced by thoughtful specification and choice of building systems. The use of PUR foam in concrete element construction, for instance, is virtually impossible to avoid due to the required size tolerances.

The choice of a variant depends in practice on the functional demands being made, such as the degree of airtightness, whether shrinking and expanding can be accommodated, and whether it is affected by the weather. The application of coconut fibre or sisal for sealing a joint on the exterior wall is only possible if the material is covered by joinery. Sealing tape made of mineral wool is supplied on a roll. Joints wider than 15 mm can be covered by a double strip. Mineral wool can also be used for base fillings in combination with a finish of elastomeric sealants.

Sealing cracks

preference 1	*preference 2*	*preference 3*	*not recommended*
EPDM and EPT-rubber	 —	 PE tape	 PVC and PUR tape

environmental preference

Rubber seals and cell tapes are suitable for sealing cracks. PE and PVC tape consist of foamed PE and PVC. The production process of PE is less polluting than that of PVC. PE is also more degradable than PVC.
Ethylene propylene diene monomer (EPDM) and ethylene propylene terpolymer (EPT) rubber seals are comparable to PE tape with regard to pollution, but they have the advantage of a considerably longer life-span.
See Part 4 for a more detailed description of the environmental impact of the materials mentioned.

not recommended

Tape foamed with (H)CFCs is not recommended because of the threat to the ozone layer. The use of CFC-free PVC tape is also not recommended in view of the considerable pollution caused by PVC.

basic selection

PE tape is included in the basic selection. EPDM and EPT rubber is the basic choice for applications such as the sealing of pivoting windows.

comments

An additional problem with PVC foam tape is that PVC and acrylic paint bond and so cannot be used together.
PE tapes can be used for cracks of maximum 10 mm. Products suitable for sealing wider joints are described under 36 *sealing joints*.

Elastomeric sealants

preference 1	*preference 2*	*preference 3*	*not recommended*
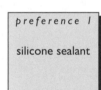 silicone sealant	 polysulphide sealant	—	 PUR sealant

environmental preference

Silicone sealant contains silicones as bonding agents, as well as filler, pigment and added substances. The toxicity of silicone sealant is determined by the drying substances and primers used, which can irritate the skin in particular. Drying substances and primers are also a problem in polysulphide sealant. In addition, lead may be present, a substance known for its toxic effects on the brain and blood. Not much is known about the toxicity of polysulphides (the bonding agent) themselves. This sealant is highly flammable, in contrast to silicone sealant.
See Part 4 for a more detailed description of the environmental impact of the materials mentioned.

not recommended

The toxicity of polyurethane (PUR) sealant comes from its polyurethane component, the primers (skin irritations) and the tin alloys used. These sealants are not recommended because the PUR component is toxic.

basic selection

Polysulphide sealant is satisfactory and no dearer than PUR sealant; the disadvantage with silicone sealant is that it is not suitable for use in all situations.

comments

Where either plastic or elastomeric sealant could be used in a particular application, then elastomeric sealant has the advantage that it is longer lasting (8–15 years) than plastic sealant (2–10 years). This leads to a reduced requirement for sealant over a determined period. Natural (plastic) sealant however is much less polluting, so that it is preferable to elastomeric sealant, despite its shorter life span.

The various sealants cannot be used as a matter of course in all cases. The use of silicone sealant for glazing, for example, is not advised on account of the strong bonding action.

Plastic sealants

preference 1	*preference 2*	*preference 3*	*not recommended*
natural sealant	water-based acrylic sealant	butylene sealant	solvent-based (acrylic) sealant

environmental preference

Natural sealants are made from renewable raw materials, with water as the solvent. The production process does not threaten the environment, and the sealant waste degrades well. Acrylic sealants do not contain organic solvents, but water does not affect health. Butylene sealants contain a bonding agent which causes little harm. Other components are fillers, pigments and hardening substances. The threat from these components is small. The toxicity is determined by the aliphatic and aromatic solvents, which are present in small quantities.

See Part 4 for a more detailed description of the environmental impact of the materials mentioned.

not recommended

The toxicity of acrylic sealant which is not water-based, is determined mainly by the aromatic solvents contained in it, which may cause headaches and have a narcotic effect. These solvents are also flammable. Remnants of acrylic monomer in the bonding agent can also have a sensitising effect. The use of these sealants is not recommended in view of the threats which the solvents pose.

basic selection

The use of water-based acrylic sealant is technically comparable to, and no more expensive than its alternatives, which form more of a threat.

comments

Natural sealant is more expensive than the other sealants.

37 Floor insulation

Ground floor insulation

preference 1	*preference 2*	*preference 3*	*not recommended*
aluminium membrane	EPS, mineral wool	foamed glass, perlite	extruded polystyrene, PUR

environmental preference

Air-filled membrane pockets are suitable for thermal insulation of the ground floor. The membrane consists of a very thin layer of polyester onto which aluminium is fixed. The production of polyester, as well as that of aluminium, demands more energy and more harmful substances are released than is the case with the production of mineral wool. However, much less material is required per m^2 in order to achieve the same insulation value. The environmental burden of the use of membranes is in the end smaller than that of mineral wool and expanded polystyrene (EPS). The aluminium membrane also forms a damp-proof layer.

The airways and skin must be protected against the irritation caused by fibres released when laying mineral wool. The production of foamed glass requires relatively more energy than EPS and mineral wool.

See Part 4 for a more detailed description of the environmental impact of the materials mentioned.

not recommended

Polyurethane (PUR) and extruded polystyrene threaten the environment considerably more than mineral wool. Damage to the ozone layer inhibits the use of (H)CFCs as foaming agents.

basic selection

Mineral wool is included in the basic selection on account of its suitability and current application. If the insulation is to be applied in the space under a suspended floor with difficult access, then we would recommend the selection of one of the other alternatives listed under preference 1 or 2.

comments

Aluminium membrane is a vulnerable material which should be handled with care. Making duct transitions, for instance, is awkward. An insulation value of U < 0.3 is required to achieve a good energy saving. The insulation value of materials such as cellulose declines sharply in a damp situation such as the ground floor. These materials are therefore deemed to be unsuitable for these applications.

133

Loft floor insulation

preference 1	*preference 2*	*preference 3*	*not recommended*
cellulose	cork	mineral wool	extruded polystyrene, PUR

  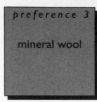

environmental preference

A loft floor can be insulated if it is not to be walked on. Advantages are the reduced consumption of material, the reduced risk of damp affecting the insulation and the simpler method of application.

Cork and cellulose have the advantage that the raw materials are renewable and that its production requires little energy and is relatively clean. As both products are degradable, they provide few problems for waste disposal. Cellulose can be produced from old paper, a waste product. If the cellulose remains visible, then clean, white, old paper can be used. The production of mineral wool uses non-renewable materials and more energy is required. The material does not degrade well either. The airways and the skin must be protected against irritation caused by fibres escaping when mineral wool is laid.

See Part 4 for a more detailed description of the environmental impact of the materials mentioned.

not recommended

Polyurethane (PUR) and extruded polystyrene cause pollution which is considerably greater than that of mineral wool. The use of (H)CFCs as foaming agents for extruded polystyrene and PUR is not recommended.

basic selection

Mineral wool is included because it is widely used and inexpensive.

37 Wall insulation

For external wallcoverings see 21–25
For external wall cladding see 31
For external wall plasterwork see 40

Insulation methods

preference 1	*preference 2*	*preference 3*	*not recommended*
cavity wall insulation	internal insulation, external wall insulation	—	no insulation

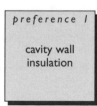

environmental preference

Cavity insulation is preferable in principle, as no wall covering or other covering is necessary and the consumption of material therefore remains limited. The insulation value that can be achieved for the external wall is limited because in most cases a cavity of only 50 mm is present. Compensation in other elements of the shell or during installation is therefore desirable from an environmental point of view.

A preference for internal or external wall insulation cannot be declared. An advantage of external wall insulation is that cold bridges can be easily resolved and prevented, as long as the various junctions and transitions are taken care of. Another advantage of external insulation is that a single, thick insulation layer can be applied, which makes it possible to achieve any desired insulation value. External wall insulation changes the appearance of the exterior considerably.

Internal insulation can give good results when carefully executed. The insulation must be transferred to the inside at the location of the support construction in order to prevent condensation caused by cold bridges. Problems arise if the floors are made of stone, concrete or brick materials. If the floor construction consists of wooden joists, then measures must be taken to prevent damage to the wood at the beam nearest the wall. Insulating the inside of the wall need not affect the appearance of the wall. Execution is not to be recommended when the building is occupied. The depth of the dwelling is of course reduced by internal insulation.

not recommended

Insulation of the external wall is also necessary in existing buildings to achieve good levels of energy saving.

basic selection

Internal and external insulation are included in the basic selection. The intervention is not low cost, but costs can be recovered and it is desirable to aim for energy savings.

comments

Inspection is recommended before a decision is made to insulate a cavity, in case it is filled with a lot of loose mortar or in case a thin insulation layer is already present in the cavity. A retrospective insulation of the cavity can create physical problems for the building in such a situation.

Applying external insulation is considerably more expensive than the alternatives. Cavity insulation is the cheapest way of insulating – when a cavity is present.

Cavity wall insulation

preference 1
perlite beads

preference 2
mineral wool

preference 3
EPS

not recommended
extruded polystyrene

environmental preference

Insulation of a cavity wall after building completion can be done with expanded clay granules, mineral wool flakes or polystyrene beads which are injected through a hole into the cavity.

Perlite beads are made of clay. The production process of perlite granules is relatively clean, the beads are fired in an oven at a temperature of 1100°C and expanded. Perlite beads need to be used in combination with other material in order to prevent the creation of cold bridges and damp through capillary action.

Mineral flakes are used for insulation after building completion; they are a waste product from the production of sheets and blankets made from mineral wool. The skin and airways must be protected against any wool fibres released when the cavity is being filled. A good seal to the cavity prevents the fibres from escaping into the dwelling. The flakes must be water repellent so as to prevent damp and a reduction in the insulation value of the mineral wool. The production process of mineral wool uses less energy and generates lower emissions than that of expanded polystyrene (EPS). This is considerably greater than that for mineral wool.

See Part 4 for a more detailed description of the environmental impact of the materials mentioned.

not recommended

Polyurethane (PUR) and extruded polystyrene threaten the environment more than mineral wool. Damage to the ozone layer inhibits the use of (H)CFCs as foaming agents.

basic selection

Mineral wool flakes are common and satisfactory as material for cavity wall insulation.

comments

No more than a maximum value of U=0.7 can be achieved by filling the cavity. It is therefore desirable to take supplementary measures, e.g. elsewhere in the dwelling shell or with regard to the installations.

Insulation of the cavity with polystyrene is a little cheaper than with mineral wool.

Internal wall insulation

preference 1
cork, cellulose

preference 2
mineral wool

preference 3
EPS

not recommended
extruded polystyrene, PUR

environmental preference

Cork and cellulose have the advantage that the raw materials are renewable, its production requires little energy and is relatively clean. As both products are degradable, they cause no problems for waste disposal. Cellulose can make use of a waste product, old paper: consideration must be given to any damp developing in the wall.

The production of mineral wool demands more energy. It does not degrade well in the

decomposition stage. Skin and airways must be protected against any wool fibres released while the product is being used.
See Part 4 for a more detailed description of the environmental impact of the materials mentioned.

not recommended

PUR and extruded polystyrene threaten the environment more than mineral wool. Damage to the ozone layer inhibits the use of (H)CFCs as foaming agents.

basic selection

Mineral wool is common and cheap and is therefore included in the basic selection.

comments

Cold bridges must be prevented when a wall is fitted with internal insulation. The insulation must be transferred about 600 mm at the party wall. This is also the case for stone, concrete or brick floors.
Insulating with cork is more expensive than other insulating materials.

External wall insulation

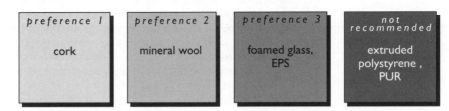

environmental preference

Cork has the advantage that the raw materials are renewable, and that the production demands little energy and is relatively clean. Cork causes no problems for waste disposal as it degrades well.
The production of mineral wool demands more energy. The waste product does not degrade well. If mineral wool is selected, then the skin and airways must be protected against any wool fibres which may be released when it is used.
The polluting properties of foamed glass are comparable to that of mineral wool. Foamed glass is bituminous-bonded however, which contaminates the foamed glass and the base with bitumen in the decomposition stage.
See Part 4 for a more detailed description of the environmental impact of the materials mentioned.

not recommended

PUR and extruded polystyrene threaten the environment more than mineral wool. Damage to the ozone layer inhibits the use of (H)CFCs as foaming agents.

basic selection

Mineral wool is included in the basic selection. Additional costs are limited compared with those incurred when using extruded polystyrene.

comments

Insulating with cork is more expensive than insulating with other materials. EPS is a little cheaper than mineral wool.

137

37 Roof insulation

Insulating a pitched roof

preference 1

cork,
cellulose,
sheep's wool

preference 2

mineral wool

preference 3

EPS

not recommended

extruded
polystyrene,
PUR

environmental preference

Cork, cellulose and sheep's wool have the advantage that the raw materials are renewable, that the production demands little energy and is relatively clean, and that the waste is degradable. Cellulose is made of old paper. More energy is required for the production of mineral wool, and it does not degrade well. Skin and mucous membranes must be protected against escaping wool fibres, which can cause irritation when working with this material.

Expanded polystyrene (EPS) poses a greater threat to the environment than mineral wool, from the extraction of petroleum, via the refining process, up to and including processing of the waste.

See Part 4 for a more detailed description of the environmental impact of the materials mentioned.

not recommended

PUR and extruded polystyrene threaten the environment more than mineral wool. Damage to the ozone layer inhibits the use of (H)CFCs as foaming agents for extruded polystyrene and polyurethane (PUR).

basic selection

Mineral wool is included in the basic selection as it is common and nearly always suitable.

comments

Cellulose can in principle only be used in situations where damp is not a problem, that is, for sloping roofs in closed box panels. The large-scale availability of cork is not guaranteed and costs are also considerably higher than for alternatives.

Insulating a flat roof

preference 1

cork

preference 2

EPS,
mineral wool,
foamed glass

preference 3

perlite

not recommended

extruded
polystyrene,
PUR

environmental preference

Cork has the advantage of being a renewable raw material, the production uses little energy and is relatively clean and the waste is degradable. Mineral wool must stand up to being walked on, when used as insulation material for a warm roof, which means that so-called 'hard-pressed' sheets must be used. The production of hard-pressed mineral wool demands more energy than the 'normal' sheets, and it does not degrade well. Skin and mucous membranes must be protected against any wool fibres escaping, which can cause irritation when working with this material. Expanded polystyrene (EPS) poses a similar

threat to the environment, from the extraction of petroleum, via the refining process, up to and including processing of the waste.
See Part 4 for a more detailed description of the environmental impact of the materials mentioned

not recommended   Polyurethane (PUR) and extruded polystyrene cause more pollution than mineral wool. The use of (H)CFCs as foaming agents for extruded polystyrene and PUR should be avoided on account of the damage to the ozone layer.

basic selection   Mineral wool sheets are included in the basic selection as this material is used regularly for this application.

comments   The method of attachment of all insulation materials is paramount for reuse of the building units at a later stage.
Large-scale availability of cork is not guaranteed. The cost of cork is considerably higher than that of the alternatives.
Expanded polystyrene (EPS) is a little cheaper than mineral wool. PUR boards in turn are more expensive than mineral wool.

Plasterwork

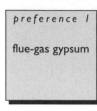

preference 1	*preference 2*	*preference 3*	*not recommended*
flue-gas gypsum	lime mortar	natural gypsum	phosphogypsum

environmental preference

Flue-gas gypsum from electricity power plants is preferable to natural gypsum and lime mortar for internal plasterwork because this gypsum is a by-product. Extraction poses no additional threat to the environment and recycling prevents the dumping of waste. Lime requires little processing, which results in a relatively pollution-free production process. Less energy is required than in the manufacture of natural gypsum mortar.
See Part 4 for a more detailed description of the environmental impact of the materials mentioned.

not recommended

Phosphogypsum, a by-product from the artificial fertiliser industry, can emit radiation. The risk of radiation from plasterwork is less than from sheets or blocks due to its limited thickness, nevertheless phosphogypsum is not recommended for plasterwork.

basic selection

Natural gypsum is included in the basic selection; it is generally available. Gypsum from power plants may also become generally available soon due to opposition being voiced about the extraction of natural gypsum in Germany.

External wall rendering

preference 1	*preference 2*	*preference 3*	*not recommended*
ceramic tiles	mineral render	synthetic render	—

environmental preference

Ceramic tiles have the advantage of a considerably longer life-span than a layer of render. They can also be separated from the insulation layer in the waste phase. Mineral render also contains synthetics, but less than synthetic render, which contains about 10% synthetics. The mixing of synthetics with stone, concrete or brick contaminates construction and demolition waste.

basic selection

Mineral render is technically comparable to synthetic render, or better, and the additional expense is negligible.

comments

Rendered external walls are generally painted. The removal of dirt and the maintenance of the paintwork means that the environment is more or less polluted, depending on the materials chosen. Mineral render attracts less dirt than synthetic render.

Fitting tiles

preference 1 bedding in mineral mortar	*preference 2* natural adhesive	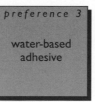 *preference 3* water-based adhesive	 *not recommended* solvent-based adhesive

environmental preference

Tiles can be fitted to a concrete base when a mineral mortar screed or render is applied (monolithic bedding). Manufacture of the screed or render does not cause much pollution and the consumption of scarce raw materials is limited, because sand forms a large proportion of the mortar.
Natural adhesives are made from natural and degradable materials. The production process of the adhesives is relatively clean.
Water-based adhesives cause pollution in their production process, however, and the waste from the adhesives is also a pollutant. A significant advantage over solvent-based adhesives is that they contain either few or no organic solvents at all.

not recommended

The toxicity of solvent-based adhesives used for fixing tiles depends on the organic solvents in particular. These solvents are flammable, and many harmful substances are released during their manufacture. The use of such adhesives, especially for large surfaces is therefore not recommended.
See Part 4 for a more detailed description of the environmental impact of the materials mentioned.

basic selection

Bedding in mineral mortar is included in the basic selection for fixing floor tiles, and water-based adhesive for wall tiles.

comments

The remnants and packaging of adhesives must be regarded as chemical waste.
Tiling walls by bedding in mortar is considerably more labour-intensive than fixing with adhesive, which makes it about 30% more expensive. This cost difference can increase when tilers are scarce.

141

Environmental selection of materials for use in Refurbishment

142

Floor screeds

preference 1	*preference 2*	*preference 3*	*not recommended*
flue-gas gypsum anhydrite	natural gypsum anhydrite	sand cement	phosphogypsum anhydrite

environmental preference

Anhydrite is a plaster mortar which is suitable for floor screeds. The environmental effects of the extraction and production of natural gypsum and the raw materials for a sand-cement mortar are comparable. The preference for anhydrite to sand cement is due to its ease of application. Anhydrite is very fluid and can be applied simply with a hose, after which it is self-levelling. The smoothing down of a sand-cement floor screed is physically hard work.

Radiation from the flue-gas gypsum is even lower than that from natural gypsum. The dumping of waste is avoided with the use of flue-gas gypsum. There is no question of extraction, in contrast to the variants, so the landscape is not affected. Anhydrite made from flue-gas gypsum therefore is preferred to natural anhydrite and sand-cement.

See Part 4 for a more detailed description of the environmental impact of the materials mentioned.

not recommended

An anhydrite floor made of phosphogypsum is not recommended due to its level of radiation.

Phosphogypsum, as well as gypsum gained from electricity power plants, is an industrial waste product. Phosphogypsum, however, can emit relatively intense radioactive radiation, whereas the radiation from the flue-gas gypsum is even lower than that of natural gypsum. Some phosphogypsum also has a high degree of heavy metals, including cadmium.

basic selection

Anhydrite made from flue-gas gypsum is included in the basic selection. It is technically uncontroversial, there are significant environmental benefits, and only limited additional costs.

comments

Anhydrite screeds can be used for suspended floor screeds and as a screed for wooden floors. There is hardly any shrinkage, there is not much risk of cracking, and the material is self-sealing.

A disadvantage of anhydrite, compared with concrete, is that the screed must be separated from the concrete floor during demolition. Concrete contaminated with plaster is not suitable for reuse as reclaimed aggregate. An anhydrite floor can be laid on top of polyethylene (PE) membrane in order to facilitate separation in the waste phase. The additional environmental burden of PE membrane is smaller than the environmental gain at this later stage.

Anhydrite floors are still somewhat more expensive than sand-cement floors. The more favourable working conditions, in particular, reduce the price difference. The fact that pouring anhydrite is faster than smoothing out a sand-cement screed contributes to this.

Bathroom and toilet floors

preference 1	preference 2	preference 3	not recommended
granitic (terrazzo)	ceramic tiles	polyester	PVC

environmental preference

A granitic floor, also called terrazzo, is a poured concrete floor to which natural stone has been added, giving the appearance of granite. The composition and finish of the floor is such that it is smooth, hard and waterproof. An advantage of a granitic floor is that no sealant is needed to make the wall junctions waterproof as the floor can have a raised lip at its edges. (This in contrast to a tiled floor.) If, however, sealant is used then the placing of the sealant is much less critical than for a tiled floor. No adhesive is required for fitting tiles. The durability of the granitic floor is greater than that of the other materials and the risk of leakage is smaller. A tiled floor is preferred to a polyester floor.

Polyester causes considerable pollution throughout its life cycle, from extraction to waste disposal. The life-span of a polyester shower floor is also limited.

See Part 4 for a more detailed description of the environmental impact of the materials mentioned.

not recommended

The use of PVC floor finish is not recommended. A PVC floor finish is vulnerable to mechanical influences, as well as being a pollutant.

basic selection

Ceramic tile finish for the floor as well as the walls is common and therefore included in the basic selection.

comments

A concrete shower floor is usually cast on a metal swallow-tail plate. The weight of a concrete shower floor usually requires strengthening of the joists.

A granite floor is more expensive than the alternatives, but the elimination of sealant and tiling results in it being maintenance-free.

143

Wall and ceiling framing systems

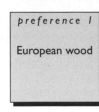

preference 1

European wood

preference 2

steel

preference 3

aluminium

not recommended

—

environmental preference

Wood is a renewable material and does not cause problems for waste disposal because it degrades well.
The extraction and production of aluminium pollutes more than that of steel, but both aluminium and steel can be reused, making the difference with native softwood less significant.
See Part 4 for a more detailed description of the environmental impact of the materials mentioned.

basic selection

Wood is included in the basic selection as a suitable material for wall and ceiling framing systems.

comments

A panelled frame for a ceiling system has the advantage that a sound-insulating layer can be applied between the panels and the ceiling. Other possible advantages are improved acoustics and disguise of existing bad ceilings.

144

Wall and ceiling panelling systems

preference 1	*preference 2*	*preference 3*	*not recommended*
flue-gas gypsum board	natural gypsum, fibreboard made of woodwool magnesite, woodwool cement or flax	sustainable plywood, mineral wool board, chipboard	phosphogypsum board

environmental preference

Flue-gas gypsum is a by-product from coal-fired electricity plants. The extraction of natural gypsum and magnesite causes environmental damage. The production of gypsum plasterboard and gypsum fibreboard uses no environmentally harmful adhesives, in contrast to the production of flax fibreboard and plywood. Bonded types of board, woodwool magnesite, woodwool cement and sustainable plywood are largely made of renewable raw materials. The regeneration of flax is greater, therefore flax fibreboard is preferred to plywood. The extraction of bonding agents for the woodwool board (magnesite and binding agents) damages the landscape.

A mineral wool board also has a sound-insulating effect. The degradability of mineral wool is poor and its fibres can irritate skin and mucous membranes when being worked with.

See Part 4 for a more detailed description of the environmental impact of the materials mentioned.

not recommended

Phosphogypsum is a by-product of the artificial fertiliser industry. The proportion of harmful substances is generally so high that the use of phosphogypsum indoors presents a risk and is not recommended.

basic selection

Natural gypsum board is included in the basic selection for the wall as well as for ceiling finishes. It is easily available and can be used at low cost.

comments

Mineral wool board, woodwool cement board and woodwool magnesite board are unsuitable for wall panels. There is a difference between gypsum plasterboard on the one hand and gypsum fibreboard on the other: gypsum plasterboard consists of a core of gypsum, which is covered with a cardboard skin on each side to strengthen it. Gypsum fibreboard, however, stands up better to mechanical forces than plasterboard. This is considered important, and so it would be preferable to use gypsum fibreboard.

Flue-gas gypsum board is about 10% more expensive than natural gypsum board. The price of natural gypsum, however, is rising due to stricter conditions being imposed on its extraction in Germany. If acoustic demands are set, then woodwool magnesite or woodwool cement panels are a good choice for ceiling panels.

145

For preservative treatments see 06
For paint work see 46
For panelling see 44

Internal joinery

preference 1	preference 2	preference 3	not recommended
European wood	chipboard, sustainable plywood	fibre cement	PVC, tropical wood

 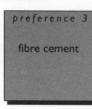 

environmental preference

Durability is not important for internal woodwork as the risk of damage by fungi or insects is minimal. Untreated softwood is satisfactory and is a renewable material which is degradable. European softwood has the advantage that its transport occurs over short distances, which keeps the energy content low.

With plywood however, harmful adhesives are used for bonding the different veneer layers together to form the material. This accounts for the material's lower ranking. The adhesive used in chipboard is also problem because even approved chipboard can incorporate an adhesive which contains formaldehyde. The risk to human health is such that the use of chipboard should be avoided for larger surfaces. There is no need to use durable wood.

See Part 4 for a more detailed description of the environmental impact of the materials mentioned.

not recommended

The use of non-sustainable wood and PVC is not recommended.

basic selection

European softwood is satisfactory and cheap, and is therefore included in the basic selection.

comments

European softwood is cheap to buy. It is commonly painted however, which is labour-intensive and damaging to the environment. This and the additional material used for painting makes it a more expensive alternative. PVC skirting boards are used particularly as a cable duct for electrical and computer cables.

External joinery

preference 1	*preference 2*	*preference 3*	*not recommended*
sustainable durable wood	painted European softwood	sustainable plywood	tropical wood, preserved wood

environmental preference

Durable woods are preferred in damp situations as they require no wood preservatives. The vulnerability of this material can be limited by proper fixing and protecting the timber ends. Less durable woods can also be used in that case. Native softwood is preferable to durable woods for applications where damp has little significance. Durable wood generally needs to be transported over longer distances, as well. The layers of veneer in plywood are bonded with harmful adhesives which determine the degree of environmental pollution it causes.

Harmful wood preservatives are not needed if the right materials are chosen and the specification is well thought out.

See Part 4 for a more detailed description of the environmental impact of the materials mentioned.

not recommended

The use of non-sustainable wood is not recommended.

basic selection

Painted softwood is included in the basic selection: it is suitable in nearly every instance, and is relatively cheap (see 46 *paintwork*).

comments

See Part 4 for examples of durable woods.

147

Environmental selection of materials for use in *Refurbishment*

148

Interior paintwork (wood)

preference 1	preference 2	preference 3	not recommended
untreated wax, water-based natural stain	water-based acrylic paint	natural paint high-solids alkyd paint	alkyd paint

Exterior paintwork (wood)

preference 1	preference 2	preference 3	not recommended
natural paint, boiled paint	high-solids alkyd paint	water-based acrylic paint	alkyd paint

environmental preference

There is no need to preserve wood which is for internal use only. A natural wax, such as beeswax, can be used if internal woodwork need to be treated. Such a wax is made of renewable raw ingredients.

A water-based natural stain has recently come on the market which is produced from renewable materials and which has a low percentage of solvents.

Water-based acrylic paints contain less organic solvents than alkyd paints (2%–7% compared with 40%–50%), but they have the disadvantage that more harmful additives, such as biocides and emulsifiers, are added in their production. The composition of the high-solids alkyd paint is comparable to that of common alkyd-resin paints. The percentage of harmful organic solvents, however, is considerably lower, being about 20%. Natural paint is mostly manufactured from renewable materials, but it does contain 30%–55% solvents, which are a threat to health; for instance there is turpentine, which particularly threatens the health of the painter when working indoors.

See Part 4 for a more detailed description of the environmental impact of the materials mentioned.

not recommended

The greatest disadvantage of commonly used alkyd paints are the organic solvents (40%–50%) which threaten the painter's health and the quality of the air.

basic selection

Natural paint and high-solids alkyd paint for interior woodwork and high-solids alkyd paint for outside.

comments

Door and window frames painted with natural paint cannot be guaranteed as can softwood frames which have been painted with an undercoat of alkyd resin paint and then a coating of water-based paints. There is no such problem with high-solid paint. Remnants of all paints must be treated as chemical waste.

Natural paints are more expensive than the alternatives because of unfamiliarity with the application and its slow rate of drying. However, manufacturers are trying to reduce the percentage of solvents.

The drying time of high-solids paint is longer than that of the commonly used alkyd paint, which can cause problems in mass production due to a lack of drying space.

Boiled paint is a favourable alternative for wooden external wall cladding (see Part 4).

Wood/stone joints

preference 1	preference 2	preference 3	not recommended
natural preservative	water-based or high-solids primer	iron red lead, alkyd resin primer	lead red lead

environmental preference

A natural preservative is preferable for the treatment of wood which is in contact with concrete, stone or brick. Natural preservatives make the wood water-repellent and protect it from attack. The preservative is relatively harmless and degradable. Primers contain harmful substances, similar to other synthetic paints, but the percentage of filler is greater and therefore the proportion of solvents is proportionally lower. The filler is not normally very harmful.

Red leads are also regarded as primers, to which lead or iron oxide have been added. The effect of the iron oxide in iron red lead is mainly visual.

A similar quality of protection can be achieved with primer based on alkyd resin. Water-based and high-solids primers contain smaller amounts of organic solvents than iron and lead red lead, but iron red lead is preferable to lead red lead because lead is harmful.

See Part 4 for a more detailed description of the environmental impact of the materials mentioned.

not recommended

Lead red lead contains a considerable quantity of lead, which is harmful to health. The use of lead is not recommended.

basic selection

A high-solid or water-based primer is included in the basic selection. The protective effect is similar to that of the more common iron red lead, and the additional costs are negligible.

149

Surface preparation (walls)

preference 1	*preference 2*	*preference 3*	*not recommended*
none	natural preservative	water-based preservative	solvent-based preservative

Interior paintwork (walls)

preference 1	*preference 2*	*preference 3*	*not recommended*
whitewash	mineral paint, water-based natural stain	natural paint, water-based acrylic paint	alkyd paint

Exterior paintwork (walls)

preference 1	*preference 2*	*preference 3*	*not recommended*
mineral paint, water-based natural stain	natural paint	water-based acrylic paint	alkyd paint

environmental preference

An undercoat is not always necessary to prevent paint from being absorbed by the wall. If one is applied, then a natural preservative is preferable because they are not very harmful and are degradable. A water-based primer contains less organic solvent, but does have a number of polluting and badly degradable components.

Whitewash is our first choice for internal wall paint. The production of whitewash comprises lime dissolved in water with no further additions. Limestone or shells must be extracted and burnt for the production of whitewash, which is a relatively clean process. Mineral and water-based paints use water as a solvent. An advantage of mineral paint is that it contains few synthetics, and it covers surfaces in a single layer so that less paint is needed.

A disadvantage with natural paints, compared with mineral paints, is that organic solvents are released which can be a threat to health when used indoors.

See Part 4 for a more detailed description of the environmental impact of the materials mentioned.

not recommended

The use of materials containing solvents is not recommended. The composition of alkyd-based wall paints is similar to that of alkyd paints for wood.

basic selection

For the preparation of walls, if necessary, use a water-based paint.
For internal walls use a water-based paint.
For external walls use a mineral paint.

comments

Whitewash is less impervious to water than to other wall paints, which can be an advantage. A disadvantage with whitewash is that it is not very smudge-proof.
Remnants of water-based wall paints must also be treated as chemical waste.
Rinsing brushes and other tools under the tap, for instance, causes a lot of pollution.

Ferrous metal paintwork

preference 1	*preference 2*	*preference 3*	*not recommended*
natural paint, duplex system	high-solids alkyd paint	alkyd paint, iron red lead	lead red lead, epoxy-alkyd systems, thermal galvanising

environmental preference

Duplex galvanising is done by applying a powder coating to a thermal galvanised layer as a finish. The powder coating is applied electrolytically in the factory, which means that no solvents are used and little paint is spilled. The life-span of a duplex galvanised coating is considered to be rather longer than that of a thermal layer of zinc. The powder coating prevents leaching of zinc to the soil. Its advantage, compared with other paint systems, is that no layers of paint need to be applied during its life-time, with a reduction in solvents. Steel could in principle be treated with alkyd or natural paint. Natural paint is made of natural raw materials, but it contains a high proportion of natural solvents.
A high-solids alkyd paint is preferable to common alkyd paint because it contains less solvent.
See Part 4 for a more detailed description of the environmental impact of the materials mentioned.

not recommended

Thermal galvanising is not recommended for outdoor use as zinc leaches when water runs over it. Leaching gets worse in aggressive environments, and the zinc layer is also vulnerable to damage, for instance when tightening fasteners. A damaged zinc layer can be painted over.
Treatment with a primer is necessary.
The use of lead red lead is also not recommended because lead is harmful to health.
Paint systems based on epoxy must be avoided due to the harmful emissions during the production process and the effects on the workers' health.

basic selection

Duplex galvanising is common, but expensive compared with the alternatives.
We have therefore included a high-solid paint as a basic alternative.

151

Environmental selection of materials for use in *Refurbishment*

**Kitchen
units/cupboards**

preference 1

European wood

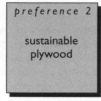

preference 2

sustainable
plywood

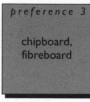

preference 3

chipboard,
fibreboard

*not
recommended*

plywood made
from tropical
wood

environmental preference

Solid, non-tropical wood has the advantage that it does not contain adhesives.
Plywood contains less adhesive and is longer-lasting than chipboard.
The bonding in chipboard poses more problems than that of the other alternatives. The production of adhesives itself releases many harmful substances. Chipboard is also faced with a synthetic layer (melamine) which impedes efficient waste disposal.
See Part 4 for a more detailed description of the environmental impact of the materials mentioned.

not recommended

The use of tropical plywood is not recommended.

basic selection

There is no basic selection as alternatives to chipboard are at present still too expensive for regular use in the construction of domestic buildings.

comments

The difference in price between kitchen units made of chipboard and those made of solid wood is typically a factor of four. This means that in practice, particularly in social housing construction, it is not financially feasible to avoid using chipboard. There is, however, some hope that affordable kitchen units will be developed which do not make use of chipboard.

152

Work surfaces

preference 1	preference 2	preference 3	not recommended
beech	granitic finish, stainless steel	synthetic resin board, synthetic stone	chipboard faced with melamine

environmental preference

Wood normally has the advantage that it is a renewable raw material, that little pollution is caused in processing and that it does not cause problems for waste disposal. A granitic working surface, also called terrazzo, is a concrete slab which incorporates a natural stone. The composition and finish is smooth, hard and waterproof. The production process of a granitic working surface is cleaner and costs less energy than that of synthetic stone and synthetic resin board. Synthetic resin bonded boards cause problems for waste disposal, unlike the other products. A stainless steel work surface can be reused at the end of its useful life. The stainless steel top is easily separated from the plywood base.
See Part 4 for a more detailed description of the environmental impact of the materials mentioned.

not recommended

Chipboard surfaced with melamine is a pollutant on account of the large quantity of bonding material used.

basic selection

A stainless steel work surface is somewhat cheaper than a synthetic resin bonded board, and is therefore included in the basic selection.

comments

Steel and synthetic resin bonded work surfaces are cheaper than those made of beech or a granitic finish. Synthetic resin bonded work surfaces seem in practice to have an advantage over other options as the occupants can choose the colour.

Wallcoverings

preference 1	preference 2	preference 3	not recommended
paper	—	—	vinyl-coated paper

environmental preference Paper is based on cellulose, which is a renewable, degradable product. The production process of wallpaper is relatively clean.

not recommended The use of vinyl wallcovering coated with PVC is not recommended.

basic selection Wallpaper is common and cheap.

comments An advantage of wallpaper is that it is easy to paint over. An advantage of vinyl wallcovering is that it can be cleaned with water.

Floor coverings

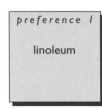

preference 1	preference 2	preference 3	not recommended
linoleum	ceramic tiles	—	vinyl

environmental preference Linoleum is preferable to tiles as a floor covering in common rooms. Linoleum consists of renewable raw materials such as cork, linseed oil and jute and its degradability is good, depending on the finish. Ceramic tiles are made of the less renewable material clay with additives for colour and hardness. They have a much greater energy content because of the firing process, but they have the advantage that they are harder and therefore less vulnerable to damage.

not recommended The use of vinyl containing PVC is not recommended.

basic selection Ceramic tiles are included in the basic selection because linoleum is too vulnerable in certain situations.

comments An advantage of floor coverings compared to a hard floor of wood or stone-like material is the sound insulation it offers. This reduces noise pollution to neighbouring houses or dwellings located below. Linoleum is more expensive than vinyl, but it lasts longer.

For lining a timber gutter see 31

Gutters

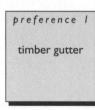 preference 1 timber gutter	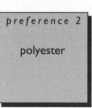 preference 2 polyester	 preference 3 coated aluminium, recycled PVC	not recommended PVC, zinc, copper

environmental preference

Timber gutters and those made of polyester, coated aluminium and PVC do not corrode. The production processes for aluminium and PVC guttering are more environmentally damaging, than those for timber and lined gutters. This is true to a lesser extent for polyester guttering. Coated aluminium guttering is long-lasting and has a high-grade reuse value. 'Recycled PVC' means that a substantial fraction has been recycled. Alternatively, future recycling should be guaranteed

not recommended

The problem with zinc and copper guttering is corrosion, leading to contamination of the waste water or soil with zinc or copper. This is harmful to water quality and organisms in particular. In addition zinc is a scarce resource and has a relatively short life. PVC roof gutters give rise to considerable pollution during the production stage and as a waste.

basic selection

A lined timber gutter is much more expensive than a polyester one. The latter is therefore recommended for the basic selection.

comments

It is possible to eliminate the use of a gutter, which is primarily the first choice. This could be done by the use of a green roof, for example, preferably combined with a large overhang. The fixing of shingle pit strips under the roof overhang is desirable. The roof overhang also has a favourable effect in that it protects the external wall woodwork. A wooden gutter construction is about twice as expensive as a polyester gutter. The copper gutter is about 20% more expensive than the polyester gutter.

155

Gutter linings

preference 1 EPDM, modified bitumen	preference 2 blown bitumen	preference 3 polyester	not recommended PVC, zinc, lead

environmental preference

The advantage of a gutter lined with ethylene propylene diene monomer (EPDM) is that it is a durable material, and the production process of EPDM is less polluting than that of blown bitumen.

The production of bituminous products causes considerable pollution, from the extraction of petroleum, via the refining process up to and including the waste disposal. However, the life-span of modified bitumen is longer and less material is needed.

not recommended

The use of PVC, zinc and lead is not recommended. Lead is an extremely toxic material for humans and the environment. The problem with zinc is corrosion leading to contamination of the waste water or soil with zinc This is harmful to water and organisms in particular. In addition, zinc is a scarce resource with a relatively short life. See Appendix 1 for a more detailed description of the environmental impact of the materials mentioned.

basic selection

A gutter lined with EPDM is included in the basic selection in view of the minimal absolute additional cost.

Drainpipes

preference 1

PE,
PP

preference 2

polyester

preference 3

steel,
recycled PVC

not recommended

PVC,
copper

environmental preference

Synthetic pipes do not corrode and their production processes are less environmentally-damaging than those of steel, copper and PVC. 'Recycled PVC' means that a substantial fraction has been recycled. Alternatively future recycling should be guaranteed. The production processes of polyethylene (PE) and polypropylene (PP) pollute least.

not recommended

The problem with copper pipes is corrosion, leading to contamination of waste water with copper. This is harmful to water organisms in particular. PVC down-pipes give rise to considerable pollution during production and as waste.

basic selection

PP can be used in all cases with negligible additional costs, compared with PVC, and is therefore included in the basic selection.

comments

PE drainpipes warp when exposed to direct sunlight and can therefore only be used in shielded locations. PP drainpipes are now available, which are resistant to ultra-violet radiation, which makes brittle pipes a thing of the past.
A PP drainpipe is about 10% more expensive than PVC drainpipes. Copper is considerably more expensive, but lasts longer and has recycling value.

Internal waste systems

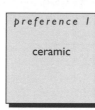

preference 1

ceramic

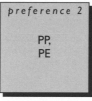

preference 2

PP,
PE

preference 3

recycled PVC

not recommended

PVC

environmental preference

The production process of ceramic pipes is considerably cleaner than that of synthetic pipes. The pipes cause few problems for disposal as waste.
Polypropylene (PP) and polyethylene (PE) score again more favourably than polyvinyl chloride (PVC) with regard to these aspects. In addition PP and PE are not bonded in contrast to PVC, but are attached with clamp connections. This not only eliminates the use of harmful adhesives, but also increases opportunities for reuse. 'Recycled PVC' means that a substantial fraction has been recycled. Alternatively, future recycling should be guaranteed.
See Part 4 for a more detailed description of the environmental impact of the materials mentioned.

not recommended

Problems with the production, as well as the waste disposal of PVC are greater than they are with PP. The use of non-recycled PVC is not recommended.

basic selection

PE and PP prove to be low cost compared with PVC and have therefore been included in the basic selection.

comments

The present generation of ceramic pipes can be used for more applications than previously because of the flexible connections used and diameters. Ceramic sewage pipes are unfortunately not available in small diameters. The prices for the alternatives differ little, although the attachment of ceramic pipes is more expensive. This is the case to a limited extent only for PP as the prevention of sagging requires a few more brackets than for horizontal pipes.

Environmental selection of materials for use in Refurbishment

157

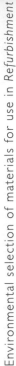

Water supply

preference 1

PE,
polybutylene,
PP

preference 2

stainless steel

preference 3

copper

not recommended

—

environmental preference

The problem with copper pipes is corrosion, leading to contamination of the waste water with copper. This is harmful to water organisms in particular. This is not offset by the fact that copper has a high grade of reusability. Corrosion also occurs to a lesser extent in stainless steel. Synthetic pipes do not corrode and their production processes are less harmful to the environment than those for copper and stainless steel.

basic selection

There are sufficient alternatives to copper water pipes.

comments

The use of polyethlyene (PE) and polybutylene for water pipes is still uncommon. Polybutylene and polypropylene (PP) are suitable for hot as well as cold water pipes. PE can only be used for cold water pipes.

158

WC suites

preference 1	*preference 2*	*preference 3*	*not recommended*
Gustavsberg WSS system	adjustable flush	choice of flush	fixed flush

environmental preference

The Gustavsberg WSS system is a WC suite with a flow enlarger, and where the waste water drainage is such that only 4 litres of water are needed per flush (see Appendix 2 for suppliers). A siphon in the horizontal pipes – which lets the total water quantity through after about 20 flushes – is needed for each 10–12 dwellings. The use of this system is especially attractive in multi-storey constructions.
A cistern in which the flush depends on the length of time the flush button is depressed, enables the user to determine the exact amount of flushing water used. Another possibility is the use of a cistern which allows a choice between 3 and 6 litres of water.

not recommended

A fixed quantity of flushing water of 6 or 9 litres leads to a waste of water. The use of PVC for the WC cistern is not recommended.

basic selection

An adjustable flushing system or choice-based flushing system with a maximum flush volume of 6 litres is included in the basic selection. The additional costs are negligible.

comments

Toilet bowls must have an adapted shape to be able to limit the flushing water quantities. The cost of a water-saving WC is approximately the same as a traditional WC.
The additional costs of the Gustavsberg system are approximately the equivalent of £65–£85 per dwelling, depending on the number of dwellings connected per siphon.

159

Taps and shower heads

preference 1	*preference 2*	*preference 3*	*not recommended*
water-saving	—	standard	—

environmental preference

Water-saving shower heads and taps with flow limiters enable a reduction of tap water and energy consumption without a loss of comfort. The measure of flow can be regulated for each respective tap. This is usually somewhat more for kitchen taps than for a washbasin tap (6–8 litres per minute compared with 5–7 litres per minute).
Some shower heads have an adapted internal design which, when combined with a built-in flow limiter, saves water without any loss of comfort.

basic selection

A water-saving shower head and water-saving tap are included in the basic selection.

comments

Flow limiters which are not vulnerable to scale are preferred in regions with hard water. We would advise using flow limiters which work independently of the pressure. However, the use of flow limiters is not possible for all types of domestic hot water installation. The tap threshold of the equipment must not fall below a certain value, because otherwise the equipment will not start.

A widespread misunderstanding is the use of perlators as a water-saving measure. Perlators introduce air into the water, giving the impression that a fuller flow is coming from the tap. In fact no saving of water occurs unless perlators are used in combination with flow limiters.

The additional costs incurred when installing water-saving taps and shower heads can be recovered within six months, where water is metered.

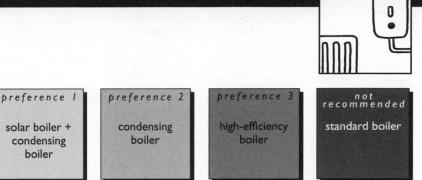

Heating installation

preference 1	*preference 2*	*preference 3*	*not recommended*
solar boiler + condensing boiler	condensing boiler	high-efficiency boiler	standard boiler

Provision of domestic hot water

preference 1	*preference 2*	*preference 3*	*not recommended*
solar boiler + condensing boiler	condensing combination boiler	high efficiency combination boiler	standard combi boiler, any electric water heating, water heater without a flue

environmental preference

A solar water-heating system achieves the greatest saving of energy. A condition, however, is that supplementary heating is gas-fired. Solar boiler installations currently on the market are suitable only for heating domestic hot water, not for space heating. The latter demands a large collector surface and a large storage tank. The problem with this is that most of the heat gain is achieved during seasons when the need for space heating is minimal.

The savings which a condensing boiler boiler provides are much greater than those of a high-efficiency. In both cases, a low-NO_x boiler is preferred on account of its less harmful emissions. It is often advantageous, from an energy-saving point of view, to choose a heating installation which also supplies the domestic hot water.

not recommended

The use of conventional boilers is not recommended. The use of high-efficiency appliances or condensing boilers is necessary in order to achieve a high level of energy saving.

The energy content of electrically-heated water is much higher than that of water heated by gas. The use of any form of electrical water heating is therefore not recommended.

basic selection

Gas-fired condensing combination boilers are included in the basic selection for space heating and the provision of domestic hot water. The cost of this boiler is still considerably higher than that of the high-efficiency boiler, but it is balanced out by savings which make up the additional cost within several years.

comments

The choice of installation depends on the circumstances.

A preference for central heating rather than localised heating cannot be given. It may be attractive to heat smaller dwellings with individual heaters. Consideration should also be given as to whether the heating power which can be gained from industrial waste present in local districts could be used, or other energy-from-waste measures.

In the Netherlands, the additional costs of a solar boiler installation in an existing building currently amount to about Dfl 3,000–4,000(£1100–£1500) per installation, including subsidies. Sometimes the distance between the location of the installation and the tap point is extremely large. A long pipe results in the loss of energy and water.

161

Insulation of pipes

preference 1 cork	*preference 2* mineral wool	*preference 3* polyether	*not recommended* extruded polystyrene, PUR

environmental preference

Cork insulation offers the advantage that the raw material is renewable, its extraction uses little energy, and it is relatively clean. The waste is also degradable.

More energy is needed for the production of mineral wool, and it degrades into harmful products. Skin and mucous membranes have to be protected if mineral wool is being applied because fibres released during this process lead to irritation. Pollution as a result of the use of polyether is less than that of PUR. A mechanical attachment of the insulation shells with wire or clips is preferable to glueing.

See Part 4 for a more detailed description of the environmental impact of the materials mentioned.

not recommended

PUR causes pollution which is greater than that of mineral wool and polyether. The use of (H)CFCs as foaming agents for extruded polystyrene and PUR is therefore not recommended in view of the damage they cause to the ozone layer.

basic selection

Mineral wool is included in the basic selection because it is a commonly used material.

comments

A reduction in the loss of heat in hot water pipes does not always balance out the extra pollution caused by the use of insulation materials, compared with central heating pipes. This is, however, the case when the pipes cross unheated spaces. Cellulose is preferable as an insulation material for service ducts not only because of the secondary characteristic of the material, but also because of its sound insulation and fire-resistant properties. To this end a flame retardant is added.

162

Mains trunking

preference 1	preference 2	preference 3	not recommended
PP	—	PVC	—

environmental preference

The production of PP is less environmentally-damaging than that of PVC. An important advantage of PP is that chlorine is not used in the product. The waste phase of PP also causes less pollution than that of PVC.

See Part 4 for a more detailed description of the environmental impact of the materials mentioned.

not recommended

The use of PVC is still unavoidable in this application (see comments).

basic selection

As no alternative for PVC is available, this building element is not included in the basic selection

comments

A manufacturer is engaged in the development of trunking made of PP.

Part 4

Environmental effects of building materials in common use

Stone, concrete, brick-like material and glass

Pollution per kilogram created by stone, concrete and brick-like material is, generally, minimal. It is the sheer quantity use of these materials used in construction that leads to the environmental problems associated with them – not because of scarcity, since technical availability is not generally an issue, but because the process of extraction of these vast quantities of stone can severely damage the landscape. In some cases the ecosystem characteristic of a particular geology is unable to recover fully after extraction has ended.

Another issue related to the use of these large quantities is the energy needed for transport at various stages – of raw materials, of semi-manufactured and finished products, and finally of demolition waste. In addition to the energy this involves additional emissions and nuisance caused by heavy transportation (noise, dust, vibration). The transport of stone forms a substantial part of total transportation, and contributes, in part, to the environmental damage caused by the infrastructure required.

Production processes are relatively simple: those frequently used are crushing, riddling, mixing, pressing, drying and baking. The emissions are mostly limited to combustion gases and dust. Drying and baking require relatively more energy.

Stone, concrete and related products last the entire life-span of a building. Demolition causes a lot of waste, which will be most likely dumped. Although such waste is for the greater part harmless (in the sense of non-toxic), problems do arise regarding use of space.

Recycling these materials provides a saving of raw materials on the one hand, and a reduction in waste on the other. Dutch building policy aims at recycling stone: waste is required to be reused as raw material. Examples of such secondary construction materials are reclaimed aggregate, fly ash, blast-furnace and industrial gypsum. The main risk is that by-products are contaminated to a greater or lesser extent. Possible consequences include extraction of heavy metals in water or an increase in the degree of interior radiation.

After demolition of buildings in which by-products are have been used, the rubble might possibly be polluted, which could make it unsuitable for future recycling. In the Netherlands, policy is currently being developed which should guarantee careful use of by-products.

Concrete

Concrete consists roughly of 53% gravel, 26% sand, 14% cement and 7% water. Gravel, cement and, to a lesser extent, sand are 'scarce' – mainly because the ecological implications of their extraction makes exploitation of all reserves impossible. The use of clean, reclaimed aggregate instead of gravel is a significant step forward. Care must be taken with the use of some by-products – for example, blast-furnace and fly ash as bonding agent substitutes.

Because of the technical quality requirements of structural concrete, the quantity of gravel that can be replaced by reclaimed aggregate is currently a maximum of 20%. Currently, therefore, concrete produced using reclaimed aggregate still consists of 42% gravel, or about 1000 kg gravel per m^3 of concrete. Current research indicates that higher percentages of reclaimed aggregate are possible, depending on the application.

The energy content of concrete itself, though low, is mainly due to its cement. content Production of Portland cement requires considerably more energy than blast-furnace cement, especially in the production of concrete clinker from marl. In addition, this process releases CO_2.

However, although concrete has a low energy content per kilogram, a reinforced concrete supporting framework comprises the greater part of the energy content of a building. This is not only due to the large quantity of concrete itself, but also to the steel reinforcement. The amount of steel used will depend on the application.

Foamed concrete and cellular concrete

With both these terms, we refer to concrete foamed using almost harmless foaming agents. Foamed concrete refers to in situ concrete, and cellular to performed blocks or other components. Both foamed and cellular concrete are supplied in various compositions, and usually consist of cement with added limestone or sand. By-products such as fly ash and blast-furnace are often used as substitutes for the cement itself, or as admixture.

Because of the low specific weight the material's energy use per unit of volume is minimal. The main environmental effects are the energy needed for transportation and emission of harmful substance if by-products are use.

Both foamed and cellular concrete are unsuitable for reuse as reclaimed aggregate in concrete, but can be reused as a filler or foundation material.

Gypsum

An important environmental effect of natural gypsum the damage its extraction causes to the landscape. However, natural gypsum can be substituted, completely or partly, by industrial gypsum. The most important industrial gypsums are flue gas (sulphur) gypsum, precipitated during gas desulphurising processes (particularly at power plants) and phosphogypsum, a by-product of the fertiliser industry.

Gypsum waste from construction is not used as secondary material.

The heavy metals and radioactive particles in flue gas gypsum are equal to or less than in natural gypsum. The amounts can be considerably higher in phosphogypsum, depending on its source. Phosphogypsum from European sources is not recommended in the construction of dwellings, because of the possibility of a high degree of harmful substances.

Glass

Glass consists of 60% silver sand, 20% sodium carbonate and 20% sulphates (including diabase and dolomite). None of the raw materials are regarded as scarce; though the supply of silver sand is considered to be limited.

The main environmental factor in glass is the large amount of energy needed to achieve the high temperatures required for processing the raw materials. Most of the emissions related to glass production come from energy production, though the melting process also releases SO_2 and fluoride.

Glass can be very successfully recycled, for some purposes, by remelting. Production of new sheet glass, however, can tolerate very little contamination by recycled glass. In the Netherlands practically all production waste is reused. Glass waste released by construction can only be recycled into low-grade glass.

Foamed glass

The raw materials for, and the first phase in the production process of foamed glass are identical to those of glass. Glass is mixed with carbon and crushed. After the foaming process the closed cells are filled with CO_2. Except for the emissions resulting from energy use, only very small amounts of CO_2 and H_2S are released.

Foamed glass is compounded with bitumen which makes it hard to separate it after demolition. The contamination of foamed glass with bitumen limits the recycling possibilities.

Glass wool

The raw materials for, and the first phase in the production process of glass wool are identical to glass. The melting process of glass wool also requires a lot of energy. After the fibring process the melted glass fibres are bound with synthetic resin and the material hardens. Both the hardening process and resin production release phenol, formaldehyde and ammonia. Nowadays, certainly in the Netherlands, glass wool is made in almost completely closed processes in which the harmful substances released are reintroduced, so the environmental impact of production is decreased.

There is a discussion about the threat posed by glass fibres. Unlike asbestos, they do not seem increased risk of cancer; however the fibres irritate the skin and mucous membranes, causing problems during installation. When working with glass wool it is important to ensure good ventilation and to wear personal protection.

Solid stone, manufactured (cast), synthetic stone

Ashlar products (stone facings) and other architectural stonework can consist of solid stone, manufactured stone, or synthetic stone. Manufactured, or cast, stone products are made of pulverised stone bonded with synthetic resin or cement. Synthetic stone is produced from minerals and synthetic resin – the quantity of resin in synthetic stone is higher than in manufactured stone.

The main environmental effect is the damage to the countryside caused by quarries and related infrastructure. Because of the large quantities, transport is an issue too.

A possible impact of manufactured and synthetic stone is that the production of bonding agents (synthetic resins) can harm human health and the environment.

In the disposal phase the differences between the various stone materials are minor.

Sand-lime brick

Sand-lime brick consists of 5% to 8% lime and 92% to 95% sand. Many types of sand are suitable, therefore the less scarce types of sand may be used. The raw materials can be substituted, in part, by materials such as fly ash.

The energy content of sand-lime brick stems mainly from the burning of the lime and the high-pressure compression involved in forming bricks, blocks or other elements. Emissions during production are minimal. Sand-lime brick is unsuitable for reuse as reclaimed aggregate in concrete, though it can be used in low-grade applications, as a filler or foundation material.

Ceramics

Clay, sometimes with additives, is used mainly for the production of ceramic materials. Ceramic tiles are glazed. Porous brick is produced by adding sawdust, which creates the cavities after incineration.

The scarcity of the raw material is the result of previous extraction. By-products such as fly ash can partly replace raw materials of ceramics. The energy content of ceramics is a consequence of the high temperatures required for firing the clay and adding a glaze. When ceramics are applied as masonry, the energy content of cement production also has to be taken into account.

Ceramics can be converted into aggregate which can, in limited quantities, be used in concrete. Currently ceramic waste is mostly reused as a filler or foundation material.????

Loam

Loam is a combination of clay and fine sand particles. It is mixed with additives depending on the application, such as straw and expanded clay granules (for insulation), or cement and lime (for water resistance). Loam can also be used in combination with a timber frame.

Loam can be found in many locations and can be extracted without much damage to the environment. The energy content of loam is low as the material is not chemically or thermally processed. Dry, hardened loam can be made malleable again by damping, and provided that no cement is added, loam is well suited for reuse. Disadvantages of loam are the labour-intensive production process and the material's sensitivity to rising damp and to direct exposure to rain and other precipitation.

Mineral wool

The raw materials for mineral wool are stone, including diabase, and blast-furnace. As in the production of glass wool, the raw materials are melted, fibred and hardened with a synthetic resin. Production emissions from mineral wool are more or less identical to those from glass wool.

Mineral wool can be recycled by compressing waste into briquettes, which can then be reintroduced into the production process. Good logistical systems are used for the collection of mineral wool waste. This form of recycling is especially beneficial in terms of reduction in the use of in raw materials and in the prevention of waste, though the melting process and the use of bonding agents still have negative effects on the environment.

Metals

The amount of mineral rock that needs to be extracting when ores are mined depends on the richness of the ores. In the mining area, the landscape and nature are seriously damaged, not only by the extraction process itself but also by changes in the groundwater level and the emission of harmful substances.

After extraction, metals are transformed into the desired products by means of various refining and production processes. Products often require a number of surface treatments before use.

Most of the environmental effects are a result of the energy required for production, and of the emission of harmful substances during surface treatment. If metals are exposed to flowing water another environmental problem occurs: metallic ions leach into the soil and water, harming a range of organisms.

An important environmental benefit of metals is their reusability. Melting down scrap is less harmful for the environment than metal extraction from ores. Reusing metals is economically attractive.

Aluminium

The most important environmental effects of aluminium occur during extraction and during conversion of the raw material, bauxite, into a semi-manufactured product. This is done electrically, demanding a large quantity of energy.

Aluminium is a material which is eminently suitable for high-grade recycling. The pollution from secondary aluminium is considerably less than that from primary aluminium, while the quality is equal. Naturally, the degree of recycling has no effect on the surface treatment, which releases harmful substances.

Steel

The extraction of coal (coke) and iron ore, and the production of steel from iron cause considerable pollution. Compared with other metals the energy content per kilogram of material is relatively low, however. An advantage of steel is its suitability for reuse, though this is less successful than with aluminium – the pollution is less compensated for than when recycling aluminium, and the percentage of secondary material is restricted. Primary reuse of steel is preferred to secondary, because work with existing steel construction requires only little repair. Sectional construction enables primary reuse.

Steel is generally provided with a surface coating, not because the release of iron particles from building elements causes damage to the environment, but because exposure to weather decreases the building elements' life-span. Zinc coatings, however, may cause problems related to the extraction of zinc particles.

Corrosion can also be avoided by using an alloy of nickel and chrome, producing stainless steel. However, that can lead to emissions of these metals during the production of stainless steel. Both nickel and chrome are heavy metals, and current environmental policy minimises their emission as much as possible.

Zinc

Depletion of recoverable zinc is expected within decades, based on current information on stock and consumption. Extraction of zinc involves emission of cadmium, which is damaging to the environment. Reduction of these cadmium emissions can only be achieved practically by limiting the use of zinc.

An important concern is the sensitivity of zinc to aggressive environments when applied outdoors. Zinc particles migrate to the soil and water from large surfaces of zinc and galvanised steel. The harm zinc causes to water organisms is currently still the subject of discussion. Another consequence of zinc's relatively quick corrosion is that zinc products which are exposed to weather influences have a relatively short life span.

Production waste from zinc is a problem. The large quantity of waste contains very high percentages of heavy metals. Recycling of zinc is possible, but is currently still too expensive to make it a viable option. At the moment the waste is stored.

Its suitability for recycling is an advantage of zinc. The zinc coating of galvanised steel products can also be easily reused. Reuse, does, however not solve the problems arising from extraction and leaching out.

Lead

Lead is a metal in extremely limited supply. Depletion of reserves is expected within decades, based on current information on stock and consumption.

An important disadvantage of lead is that it is hazardous. Production, outdoor use of lead sheet and lead paint all cause pollution through the release of lead particles.

An advantage of lead is that it is reusable. Almost all lead sheet is already recycled.

Copper

The use of copper in pipes and outdoors causes large quantities of particles to come into contact with soil and water, and pollution occurs. Copper can kill water organisms. Unpreserved copper will form a protective coating, verdigris, which resists weather influences very well. The life span of copper products is consequently very long.

An advantage of copper is that it can be recycled. Pipes and other copper products are reused on a large scale because it is economically attractive.

Synthetics

The basic raw material of synthetics is petroleum. Disasters during extraction and transport of oil petroleum often harm vulnerable and valuable ecologies. The amount of petroleum used annually is enormous: despite many known sources, depletion is expected within decades. Only a small part of the petroleum consumption (4%) is used for the production of synthetics, however.

In refineries petroleum is split in a number of basic particles. This requires energy and causes the emission of organic hydrocarbon. Important semi-manufactured products used in manufacture of synthetics are ethylene, propylene, benzene and styrene. Conversion of these semi-manufactured products into raw synthetics often requires several processes, most needing energy and causing releases of organic hydrocarbon and waste.

Sometimes semi-manufactured products of different origin are required, and their production also has detrimental environmental effects. It is often the addition of harmful substances that gives synthetics their specific qualities.

In general, synthetics involve only minor problems during the construction phase and use. Problems do occur after demolition, however, as dumped synthetics are rarely degradable and additives such as heavy metals may leach out. Though energy can be gained by incineration of synthetic waste, incineration can result in environmentally harmful emissions, depending on the synthetic, the additives and the quality of the incineration plant.

Many synthetics can be recycled successfully. These so-called thermoplastics can be remelted into basic granulate materials. An important prerequisite is that the recyclable waste is pure.

Contamination leads to reduction in quality, making synthetic waste useless for high-grade recycling. Besides thermoplastics, construction often uses elastomers (rubbers). High-grade recycling of elastomers is not yet possible. Reuse is carried out by crushing waste into granulate that can be used as filler.

PE, PP (polyethylene, polypropylene)

Polyethylene and polypropylene are simple synthetics. They are obtained from the semi-manufactured products ethylene and propylene. The additional pollution of this conversion (polymerisation) is minimal. After conversion only a few, relatively harmless, additives are submitted.

Polyethylene and polypropylene are thermoplastics and, because of their minimal variation in structure, very well suited to recycling. In case of pollution a quality loss can occur. Due to their structure and purity, incineration of these synthetics will release hardly any harmful substances.

PVC (polyvinyl chloride)

The most important raw materials for polyvinyl chloride are petroleum and salt (in the form of chloride). Chloride is extracted from salt by means of electrolysis. PVC does not require much petroleum, so has a low energy content. Its production process causes environmental problems related to electrolysis, which releases harmful substances such as asbestos and mercury. Also the storage and transport of chloride involve a risk of accidents.

The extraction of PVC from ethylene and chloride releases mutagenic materials (dichloro-ethylene, vinyl chloride), which may cause continuous harmful emissions. Although such emissions have decreased considerably in the last few years, production leads to chemical waste that contains organic chloride. High-quality PVC requires many additives, amongst others softeners, especially in soft PVC. Currently the harmfulness of such softening agents is the subject of discussion. Many of the other additives contain heavy metals. Because PVC contains chloride, incineration may result in harmful emissions of, for example, HCl, dioxin and polychlorobiphenyl (PCB).

Other waste also contains chloride, however, so it is hard to establish for which part of the pollution PVC is responsible. Dumped PVC is scarcely degradable and may produce emissions of harmful additives, e.g. heavy metals.

By recycling PVC problems of waste disposal and the polluting initial phases of the production process can be avoided. PVC can be recycled successfully. In practice, PVC varies in structure (due to quantities and additives), and the mixing that occurs in recycling results in a decrease in quality.

Consequently primary raw material is needed. Only through use of high percentages of secondary materials can the environmental effects of PVC be reduced: there are already some examples of such products. To ensure future recycling of PVC, accurate collecting systems are being developed for certain PVC products.

Bitumen

Bitumen is obtained from specific petroleum types. It contains a minimum of polycyclic al aromatic hydrocarbon. Blown asphalt-bitumen is often applied for roof covering. The blowing process effects the release of large molecular compounds of hydrocarbon and vapour, but does not release SO_2, NO_x or hydrocarbon. Asphalt-bitumen requires the addition of organic (jute, wool) or inorganic (glass membrane, polyester) reinforcement. Bitumen is often incorrectly compared with tar, which was formerly often used for roof covering. Bitumen and tar differ considerably. Tar is obtained from coal or petroleum particles which cause pollution and has, among other components, a high content of polycyclical aromatic hydrocarbons, which are carcinogenic.

Bitumen can be reused easily, though in practice bitumen is not yet recycled because of pollution of the material. Many roofs are still covered with tar, but mixture of tar waste and bitumen waste should be avoided. Instead, tar should be treated as chemical waste, separately.

APP- and SBS-modified bitumen

APP bitumen requires the addition of 30% atactic polypropylene (thermoplastic), SBS bitumen 8%–12% styrene-butadiene-styrene (elastomer or rubber). Polypropylene is a synthetic which causes relatively minimal environmental effects; the production of styrene-butadiene-styrene is environmentally more harmful. The addition of a polymer increases flexibility, elasticity, flood-resistance and strength, and extends the bitumen life-span. SBS bitumen needs to be protected against UV radiation. Altogether the environmental impact of APP and SBS bitumen is about equal.

EPDM (rubber or elastomer)

Ethylene propylene diene monomer (EPDM) polymers are extracted from the monomers ethylene, propylene and mostly cyclopentadiene. Monomers and polymers cause minimal harm to the environment.

Rubber is obtained by vulcanising polymer chains, converting a soft plastic substance into a strong elastic material. The elastomer (raw rubber) is combined with various additives such as fillers, softeners (paraffinic oils), process regulators, fire retardants, blowers and pigments. The necessary organic solvents for treatment of the semi-manufactured products can harm human health and environment.

After vulcanisation rubber resists the ageing process well, though a disadvantage is that it cannot be remelted. Recycling is possible by grinding and reusing the resulting granulate as a filler. This, however, requires a lot of energy and is a low-grade form of recycling. EPDM roof covering may, depending on the fixing and surface, be suitable after demolition for primary use in another building.

PUR (polyurethane)

As with other synthetics, part of the pollution caused by PUR is a result of the extraction of petroleum and production of semi-manufactured products in the petroleum industry. Its main raw material besides petroleum is natural gas. Polyurethane is obtained by polymerisation of isocyanate and polyol. Isocyanate is extremely harmful to human health (as was demonstrated in the Bhopal disaster). Additives are catalysts, amine and tin agents, stabilisers, pigments and fire retardants, several of which are also hazardous.
The polyurethane is then aerated into foam, with addition of blowers such as chlorofluorocarbons (CFCs and HCFCs), dichloromethane or CO_2. The use of (H)CFCs affects the ozone layer, dichloromethane involves health risks for, in particular, the production workers. The use of PUR also has environmental effects during waste disposal. It is often hard to separate from buildings, for instance when used in roofing sheets or as a crack sealant.

EPS (expanded polystyrene), extruded polystyrene

Similarly to other synthetics, part of the pollution from polystyrene is a result of the extraction of petroleum and production of semi-manufactured products in the petroleum industry. The production of EPS and extruded polystyrene out of semi-manufactured products leads to emissions of styrene and benzene. The production of extruded polystyrene requires more energy than that of EPS. Sometimes halogenated fire retardants are added to EPS and extruded polystyrene.
EPS does not require chlorofluorocarbons (CFCs or HCFCs). Pentane is generally used for the expanding process. In 1994 (H)CFC was still used for blowing extruded polystyrene.
Recycling of production waste is possible and will take place in the Netherlands in the future. Recycling of demolition waste is technically feasible but is not yet in practice.

Wood

The most important renewable raw material used in construction is wood. Little processing is needed to convert this raw material into a usable product, which makes the production process a relatively clean one, using little energy. Wood can have a number of disadvantages however, the gravity of which depends on the type of wood used and its origin. Aspects significant from an environmental point of view when selecting wood are:
– forestry management
– the need for preservatives
– transport distance

Sustainable wood

Sustainable wood is wood from plantations or forests with sustainable forestry management.

Durable wood

Durable wood is wood from Classes I and II (see table). This wood does not need any kind of preservative. Where the moisture is controlled by careful specification and regular maintenance, wood from Class III may also be used.

I Tropical wood

Use of tropical wood is not necessarily so environmentally harmful that it has to be avoided – in fact, arguments against tropical wood from sustainably managed forests hardly exist (one disadvantage, however, is that tropical wood needs to be transported over large distances). Forestry in non-tropical areas can also lead to exhaustion and deterioration of ecosystems. It is best, therefore, to be well informed before making a choice about what kind of wood to use.

The problem with tropical wood at this moment is that little tropical wood originates from sustainably managed forests. For clarity, the handbook uses the term 'tropical wood' to mean tropical wood that does *not* come from sustainable forestry. Many efforts are underway to stimulate timber-exporting countries to take measures to improve forestry management. At the time of writing, there is one approval marking system, by the Forest Stewardship Council (FSC). Other than this there is no guarantee that tropical wood is indeed from well managed forests, even if that claim is made.

2 North American, Siberian and Australian wood

Forests in these areas are often not well managed. Often wood originates from primary forests with unique ecosystems. A start at introducing better managed forestry has been made in North America and Australia, though in Siberia the situation looks worse. Again, it is better to be well informed before making a choice. The FSC mark is also anticipated for these areas.

3 European wood

Forestry management in Europe and Scandinavia is relatively advanced. Another important advantage is the reduced distances for transport. However, relatively few types of durable wood are found in Europe. In this handbook the words softwood, native softwood, deciduous wood, European softwood and pine are used. In each case this means wood from Europe. In practice this will often be timber from sustainably managed forests.

Durability class	South-and Middle America, Africa, Asia	North America, Siberia, Australia	Europe
I	azobé, iroko, bangkiria	jarrah	
II	merbau	redwood, red cedar, karri	robinia (acacia), Spanish chestnut, oak
III	dark red meranti	Oregon pine, larch, deal	deal, larch, cherry, Douglas fir
IV	okoumé	Carolina pine, hemlock	pine, spruce (fir), deal
V	ramin	–	beech, poplar

Finishes (board materials)

Board materials consist of carriers and bonding agents. Most carriers (fibres, veneers) are made of renewable raw materials, with both organic (natural or synthetic resins) and inorganic (plaster, magnesite, cement) materials used as bonding agents. Not only the composition, but also the various production processes strongly determine the characteristics of board materials.

Plywood, OSB (oriented strand board), MDF (medium density fibreboard), chipboard

Plywood, OSB, MDF and chipboard are mainly produced from renewable raw materials (wood or flax). The veneer layers used in plywood require round timber. Production of veneer produces relatively large amounts of residual waste, and this is suitable for low-grade recycling. For the production of chipboard low-grade wood qualities (residual and waste woods) suffice, which contributes to efficient use of the raw material. OSB requires higher-quality raw material (wood chips) than chipboard.

Compared with solid wood, the main disadvantage of board materials like chipboard, plywood and OSB is the use of bonding materials. The percentage of bonding materials can differ considerably, depending on the quality of the board material being produced.

The production process of organic bonding agents results in pollution. When the product is in use, harmful substances such as formaldehyde can be released in dwellings. Certificated chipboard does not carry this risk of contamination as it contains minimal formaldehyde ($<6mg/m^3$). Nowadays chipboard is available which does not release formaldehyde from the bonding agents ($<2mg/m^3$).

The life spans of the various types of chipboard vary considerably compared with other materials. High degrees of humidity or mechanical loadings shorten the life span. Plywood, OSB and, if applicable, cement fibreboard are to be recommended in these cases.

Cement, wood wool magnesite and gypsum fibreboards

Minerals are used as bonding agents in cement fibreboards. The bonding material (cement) content is approximately 25%. The environmental issues are the energy required (in particular by the cement industry) and the environmental damage caused by the extraction of raw materials.

Synthetic resin board

Synthetic resin board consists of a carrier with bonding agents. It is mostly made out of layers of paper, though a new kind of synthetic resin board consists of wood fibres taken from wood waste or recycled board material, which is a significant improvement.

Compared with other board materials, such as plywood, synthetic resin board requires more energy for production and a higher amount of bonding agent, e.g. 30% phenolic resin. An advantage is that synthetic resin boards are more damp-resistant, which results in relatively low maintenance costs for paintwork. They are also more resistant to damage than, for example, cement fibreboards.

Paints

There are many types of paint, with various compositions. Paint consists of bonding agents, solvents, fillers and additives. Additives are, for example, pigments, drying agents, polishers and anti-foaming agents.

An important environmental aspect of many paints are organic hydrocarbons, mostly released during application. They harm the health of painters and of the occupants of buildings, and contribute to an increase in the concentration of organic hydrocarbon in the atmosphere. Organic hydrocarbons react with NO_x to causes smog.

All paints contain additives harmful to human health and the environment. Pigments may contain heavy metals. Incinerating or dumping painted materials releases many of these harmful elements. Contaminated painting equipment (paintbrushes, paint-tins) and cleaning liquids also negatively effect the environment.

Alkyd paints

Alkyd paints contain alkyd resin as the bonding agent. Both 'traditional' paints and high solids are alkyd paints. With alkyd paints organic hydrocarbons are used as solvents.

Acrylic paints

Acrylic paints have acrylic resin as the bonding agent. The amount of organic solvents in acrylic paint is reduced to +10%. Acrylic paints use water as the main solvent, which explains the name 'water-based acrylic paint'. A disadvantage of acrylic paints is, however, that they contain many harmful substances, such as biocides, anti-corrosion agents and emulsifiers.

High solids alkyd paint

Other paints with lower degrees of organic solvents than the traditional alkyd paints are high solids. Environmental gain is obtained by decreasing the total amount of solvents. The amount of additives is comparable to the traditional alkyd paints, but the proportion of solid materials in high solids paint is greater.

Natural paints

An advantage of natural paints is that the raw materials are mostly of vegetable or animal origin. This is in contrast to the other types of paint, which have petroleum as the main raw material. Waste from natural paints is generally degradable. Natural paints also contain organic hydrocarbons as solvents, comparable to synthetic solvents in terms of environmental harm.

Boiled paint

A little-known natural paint is so-called 'boiled paint', made by boiling grains for a long period. It contains iron sulphate as a preservative, as well as water and natural pigments. The paint causes little pollution. Boiled paint is used in the Nordic countries in particular to protect (unplaned) gable woodwork. It is applied in one coat, without primer, and lasts 10–30 years depending on the circumstances. Boiled paint is, unfortunately, less suitable for paintwork on window and door frames.

Sealants

The composition of sealant resembles that of paint. It consists of bonding agents, solvents, fillers and additives. Important differences are the amounts of bonding agents and fillers. Many sealants contain additives (primers, hardeners) which are toxic or can lead to sensitivity reactions. Such reactions can also be caused by bonding agents such as acrylic sealant, which contains acrylic monomer. Sealants may involve a harmful production process (polyurethane sealant) or have environmental effects during demolition.
Natural sealant is completely or partly made from renewable materials and its production has hardly any environmental impact. As with paints, there are sealants with harmful organic hydrocarbons as solvents, and water-based sealants. Additives in sealants can also contain heavy metals.
Materials released during demolition can be contaminated with sealant, which makes recycling more difficult. Sealant itself is not reused, though in the Netherlands empty sealant tubes are more often collected and recycled.